Undomesticating GOD

BY JENNIFER O'SULLIVAN

31 PUBLISHING

A DIVISION OF 31 OILS, LLC

www.31oils.com

UNDOMESTICATING GOD *by Jennifer O'Sullivan*

Published by 31 Publishing
a division of 31 Oils, LLC
Aliso Viejo, California

Thank you to my editors for their support and care!
Tara Adams (Technical Editor)
Tiffany Oesch (Content Editor)

ISBN: 978-1-7344993-7-7

Printed in the United States of America

January 2020

"My appeal is addressed to those who have been previously taught in secret by the wisdom of God. I speak to thirsty hearts whose longings have been wakened by the touch of God within them, and such as they need no reasoned proof. Their restless hearts furnish all the proof they need."

A. W. Tozer

The Pursuit of God

CONTENTS

INTRODUCTION

I have been found guilty of consistently shaping God to fit neatly into my own standards, ideals, and morals. By doing so, I have stolen from God the very thing He asked me not to: His divinity. He said I am to have no other gods before Him, yet I find myself, along with others, worshiping at the feet of a host of well-disguised gods: our jobs, our kids, our spouses, even the houses, cars, and clothing we buy. In their own unique way, each has become an object of worship that supplants the place of the one True God.

A quick audit of where I spend my time and money has helped reveal the things that are most important to me. In the small imperfect corner of the world I live in, South Orange County, California, one of the largest, most indulgent idols that has been placed ahead of God, even in Christian circles, is our children. I watch as moms and dads run themselves ragged working double jobs to pay for all of the sports and after school activities and then run themselves more ragged trying to keep up by driving their kids all over the place, while succumbing to their every desire and need.

The thought of letting God be fully who He said He is can be incomprehensible to a society of self-indulgent, self-sufficient, and self-centered people-pleasers. I fear that I fear man more than I fear God. I see people clamor to be seen by their friends and family as the best. It is seemingly important to have the best kids, the best vacations, the best decor in their homes, and to drive the latest and greatest cars. I could easily shake my head and wag my finger at them, but I am guilty too! I used to think I was immune from being *that* kind of person, but I had to take note of some subtle ways selfishness crept into my own life.

Not only was I selfish in the "things" I desired, but also in how I responded to the relationships in my life. You see, I am not the best at allowing others to help, even when I need help. I had to really think about the last time I allowed someone to help me. I would often play the martyr who helped everyone else, yet felt always forgotten when it came to my needs. I had to consider that not asking for help, or worse, turning down a helping hand, was stealing joy from the other person. That broke my heart. I love helping people, and I had to consider what it would feel like if every time I tried to help someone, they simply said, "No thanks, I've got it." Not allowing people to help me was a self-absorbed thing to do, and I was doing it all of the time.

Unfortunately, as I continued down the road of a selfish life, I was dangerously stepping into the habit of trying to steal the very throne of God. I was, in essence, stating that I was fine without God. I noticed that others around me lived this way too. It was normal, almost expected. Without question, Christians are often tempted to exile God into a small corner of life's attic, only pulling Him out when they need Him. God's throne is not meant to take up a small space in a Christian's life, it is meant to infiltrate every area of it. Many of us who identify with Christianity have successfully, willfully, and woefully domesticated God.

guilty

→ I PRAY for Elisabeth AND Emmy ...
PLEASE God .....

8

The increasingly postmodern culture we live in has new pillars with weak foundations that are trying to bury God. Tolerance, individualism, and the "you-be-you" movement are but prime examples. Generation Z (those born between 1996 and 2010) is a group of people who have been immersed in the internet and social media since early childhood. They support movements like "speak your truth," transgender rights, and women's empowerment. They have even created new words for sexuality such as pansexual, which means there are no limits to one's sexuality. Interestingly, Gen Z, in some circles, is considered the least religious generation to date. They have pushed God so far off of His throne for the sake of tolerance.

Domesticating God is something that is so easy to do that it can seep into your routine without you even realizing it. Like a small fracture in a rock, over time and with the right weather conditions, the crack can expand into a huge crevice. If you set sail for a destination and your compass is off by even one degree, in the beginning of the trip it will not be too hard to correct, but if you wait until the end, the correction will require a wholesale change. You will have sailed so off course that you will end up in a completely different location, far, far away from where you intended. Ive done this for the past 7 years!

My point in writing this book is to help you make your heart sing! I want you to be so sure about your salvation, and so in love with Jesus that you desire more and more to seek Him. While I know some areas I will discuss may be hard (as they were hard for me too) I know that the higher we all raise our view of who God is, the more we will be able to love Him the way He desires us to: with all glory to Him, all praise to Him, and all honor to Him. My pastor, Ric Rodeheaver, once said, "One of the antidotes to hypocrisy is to deliberately surround yourself with other Christians so that they may lovingly challenge you." I am asking for the privilege of challenging you toward a more expansive view of Christian discipleship.

If you desire to live in God's design, there is support for you to help you make those corrections. My intention for this book is to help you in every way I can so you can do everything in your power to make certain you are going in the right direction, to the right destination. God was clear about His plan and your role in it. If you are reading this wondering what that may be, then you are in the right place. Undomesticating God is a correction that needs to be made. God never intended for us to try to domesticate Him, and luckily for us, His plan is perfect and He is sovereign. There is nothing we, as humans, can do to disrupt His plan.

~ Jen O'Sullivan

AUTHOR'S TESTIMONY

"Not everyone who says to me, "Lord, Lord," will enter the kingdom of heaven, but the one who does the will of my Father who is in heaven. On that day many will say to me, "Lord, Lord, did we not prophesy in your name, and cast out demons in your name, and do many mighty works in your name?" And then will I declare to them, "I never knew you; depart from me, you workers of lawlessness."
Matthew 7:21-23 ESV

I got my "Ticket into Heaven" at the age of 14 right before my 9th grade year. It was in 1987 at Forest Home Summer Camp. I was excited to be "in" with my church group and I quickly got involved in leadership, became a leader on the worship team, and went on several mission trips. I loved my friends and loved my church group.

But things never seemed right somehow. I searched for more knowledge and understanding. I was a good girl on most counts, at least better than others, or that's what I told myself. I loved Jesus and was told He loved me too. Outwardly I professed Christ and looked the part. I was a "Christian." I went to church, prayed, read my Bible, gave money to the church, served, and even taught in the junior high and high school ministries.

But, still, something seemed to be missing. In my late thirties, a friend of mine shared with me a story of a young woman who was brought up in the church and had "always

11

been a Christian." When she was asked to take a look at her fruits of salvation she honestly couldn't think of anything. She hadn't really grown as a Christian. Sure, she served and read her Bible, prayed, and did all the things Christians do. She even loved Jesus, but inwardly she was discontented with her life, bitter toward her husband, jealous of what others had, selfishly desired more, was lonely all of the time, and felt misunderstood and mistreated by others. She kept stuffing her life with all sorts of things to fill the emptiness she felt, not realizing the shape of the hole was a God-shaped hole that only He could fill.

That young woman could have *been* me. I realized that I never fully submitted to the lordship of Jesus. I realized that my god was so small that I had made him into my own buffet pick-and-choose religion that worked in *my* life and did not disrupt *my* plan.

I started really looking into my fruits. What are they? Are they the Fruits of the Spirit or do they go beyond that? What I found was profoundly upsetting. I was sadly misguided and misled. I was brought up in a church whose teachings were contradictory to those of the Bible. I started to attend a new church and the pastor, Dr. Mike Fabarez, said to me during this confusing time of evaluating my salvation that "the best way to guard yourself against heresy is to read your Bible thoroughly and often."

So I dug in. I allowed the Bible to teach me. I allowed God to teach me, rather than man. God placed a deep desire in me to seek Him out. I had an insatiable appetite for His Word and His true teaching. I started learning Hebrew and Greek because I wanted to understand the original context of the words that were used. What I found was startling. Major passages that I was taught meant something very different when I read them in the right context. The words that were used sometimes had different meanings to the original reader than what they mean to us today.

I learned that the reason my relationship with God never seemed right somehow had to do with my view of God. An interesting observation by A.W. Tozer states, "What comes into our minds when we think about God is the most important thing about us." I looked at God as my Daddy, a big happy grandpa in the sky. Jesus was my friend, the guy I could turn to when I really needed help. This is not what the Bible teaches about God! Sure I can turn to Jesus, but that is only a fraction of who He should be to me. I WANT HIM To "Fix" Things

This low view of God is exactly where Satan wants us all to be. Think about it. If you were given 6,000 years to perfect the art of playing the piano, you would be the best pianist ever. Satan has had over 6,000 years to perfect the art of deception with humans. Why would he be obvious? His greatest accomplishment would be to get droves upon droves of people *thinking* they are saved, all the while sending them straight to hell.

Satan and the other fallen angels are fuming mad. They don't have a chance for salvation. But we do. They are doing everything they can to get us to lower our view of God. While God reveals Himself in many ways throughout the Bible, the healthy tension between His holiness and His tenderness has fallen into disrepair. It appears that many Christians

13

have lost the capacity to understand God's terrifying majesty in an effort to make Him more approachable, like a Daddy or a familiar friend at a coffee shop. We need to keep the tension, and thereby, a corrective toward holiness might be what is needed. Think about the times the Bible mentions an encounter with God and that person feels the weight of His holiness. It's intense... really intense. Thoughtfully read through the following verses:

"And I said: "Woe is me! For I am lost; for I am a man of unclean lips, and I dwell in the midst of a people of unclean lips; for my eyes have seen the King, the LORD of hosts!" (Isaiah 6:5 ESV)

"And they were filled with great fear and said to one another, "Who then is this, that even the wind and the sea obey him?" (Mark 4:41 ESV)

"But when Simon Peter saw it, he fell down at Jesus' knees, saying, "Depart from me, for I am a sinful man, O Lord." (Luke 5:8 ESV)

I imagine that when I meet God for the first time, my body and face will be flat on the ground as low as I can get, in awe and submission to a Holy God.

"Not everyone who says to me, "Lord, Lord," will enter the kingdom of heaven, but the one who does the will of my Father who is in heaven. On that day many will say to me, "Lord, Lord, did we not prophesy in your name, and cast out demons in your name, and do many mighty works in your name?" And then will I declare to them, "I never knew you; depart from me, you workers of lawlessness." (Matthew 7:21-23 ESV)

This passage in Matthew 7 is about the people who think they are saved! He is talking about the Day of Judgment. The part about prophecy and casting out demons was what threw me off. Even though our works are different today than they were in the New Testament times, the application is the same. We have to remember the context of the time it was written. If it were written today it might say, "Lord, Lord, you're my buddy, we are super close! Did I not go to church, invite my friends, help my fellow brothers and sisters, and give tons of money to charities in your name?" The sentiment is exactly the same, just in the context of our day.

I don't know about you, but I just cringe at this. This is quite possibly the most horrifying passage in all of scripture. Think about how many millions of people are deceived into thinking they are saved but are not. Jesus says on that day *many* will question why they are cast into hell. This is no light matter. THIS IS HUGE!

I have heard people claim that Matthew 7:21-23 is about non-believers or people who loosely identify with Christianity but who aren't actually saved. This would be a gravely incorrect assumption and here's why. When speaking directly to a person, saying their name twice, according to the Hebrew tradition, is not only a point of importance, but a form or intimacy.

The people depicted in Matthew 7 said, "Lord, Lord". They thought they had an intimate relationship with Jesus. I was one of these people! I thought I had an intimate relationship with Jesus. I was emotionally connected; or so I thought. How devastating that Jesus simply says to them, *"I never knew you; depart from me, you workers of lawlessness."* Talk about a slap in the face. More like an eternal slap of doom. When the Holy Spirit got ahold of my soul, this one realization of how blind I was caused me to try to understand exactly how this deception could happen, and if there was any way possible to help others.

"I know your works: you are neither cold nor hot. Would that you were either cold or hot! So, because you are lukewarm, and neither hot nor cold, I will spit you out of my mouth. For you say, I am rich, I have prospered, and I need nothing, not realizing that you are wretched, pitiable, poor, blind, and naked." (Revelation 3:15-17 ESV)

This is a letter to the church in Laodicea. It was a thriving church back in Paul's day, but is no longer a physical church or town. Laodicea is often considered, by Bible scholars, to represent the current church we live in. I mistook the various ministries I was involved in as fruits when all of my efforts were really just self-promotion. I was living a selfish and self-serving kind of faith in Jesus, only trusting in Him when I *needed* Him. I was the epitome of a "Lukewarm American Christian" living out a clinical sort of faith.

I realized that it is not us who chooses God, but it is God who mercifully chooses us. I got so wrapped up in asking why God would save some people and not others. The question really should be, why does He save *anyone* at all? We are *all* a mess. *All* of us are unworthy. *All* of us are sinners... *ALL!*

"For while we were still weak, at the right time Christ died for the ungodly. For one will scarcely die for a righteous person—though perhaps for a good person one would dare even to die—but God shows his love for us in that while we were still sinners, Christ died for us. Since, therefore, we have now been justified by his blood, much more shall we be saved by him from the wrath of God. For if while we were enemies

we were reconciled to God by the death of his Son, much more, now that we are reconciled, shall we be saved by his life." (Romans 5:6-10 ESV)

With the understanding that was brought to me by the Holy Spirit, and by God's mercy by opening my eyes, on May 20, 2013, I came to the harsh realization that I had been only "dating Christ" and not actually committed to Him in every way He commands us to be. When I say "dating Christ," I mean I allowed Him into my life on my terms, like a co-pilot rather than *the* pilot of my life. It was then that I got on my knees and fully repented of my arrogance and sinful foolishness, gratefully handing over my entire life to Him.

Since that day there have been several significant changes in my life. Outwardly, my life was characterized by my selfishness and desire for things of this world. It was astounding to see the supernatural work of the Holy Spirit placate these self-indulgent desires almost overnight. God says, *"Do not love the world or the things in the world. If anyone loves the world, the love of the Father is not in him."* (John 2:15 ESV) I remember working so hard for my sports car that I purchased. When I woke up that next morning on May 21, 2013, the day after giving my life to Christ, and went into the garage, literal bile came up in my mouth when I saw the car. It represented a huge portion of my sin and I wanted nothing to do with it anymore.

My life was also characterized by an inward disdain for humanity as a whole. Even though my friends didn't see this, I felt I was somehow better than everyone else; more entitled than others, smarter somehow. I can honestly say that my heart of stone has been turned to a heart of flesh with compassion and love for everyone! God is clear: *"By this all people will know, that you are my disciples, if you have love for one another."* (John 13:35 ESV)

Another important area where I was changed is that I am not ashamed of Jesus anymore. The boldness of others for Christ is something I always marveled at and just thought, "That's for them but not for me." I was embarrassed to pray in public areas, foolishly thinking it made Christians look weird. I was a "Christian" who would tell others that my faith was for me alone and that they were on their own journey. I never shared who Jesus was with others unless they directly asked me. The Bible says, *"I am not ashamed of the gospel, for it is the power of God for salvation to everyone who believes!"* (Romans 1:16 ESV) Now I am always looking for ways to insert Jesus into the conversation.

Since that day, people often ask me if I am sure that I was actually saved in 2013 and not back in 1987, with the years in between just being part of my sanctification process like a sort of renewal of faith or a prodigal child scenario. Looking back on the years since I became a true Christian, I can tell you with 1,000 percent assurance that I am NOW saved and I was NOT saved as of May 19th in 2013, the day before my actual conversion. There was no repentance and no real conversion of giving my life to Jesus prior to May 20th. It is something I have spent a lot of time tracking, wrestling with God about in prayer, and practicing a sensitivity to receiving the Holy Spirit's instruction to be certain on this point.

Now I can count so many fruits that are solid evidence that I am actually saved. I have kept track of all the fruits I have found in the Bible that are not just the Fruits of the Spirit. One area that stands out as clear evidence of conversion is the discipline of God. Would you ever feel comfortable harshly and firmly disciplining your neighbor's child? Would they get the same punishment as your own child? No! Certainly not! In the years since my conversion, I have had the privilege of getting disciplined (sometimes harshly) on a few occasions by my Father. While not fun, I see the beauty in His discipline. What a picture of correction, love, and assurance.

There aren't any physical skills you need to learn or clothing you need to wear to become a Christian. Becoming a Christian, in human terms, is not hard. *Being* a Christian, on the other hand, is much harder than I would have ever thought because it means denying the very thing you have never had to deny: yourself. We are guaranteed hardships in this life. I laugh at how easy life was before my salvation, but I would not have it any other way. I have lost my career, lost family members, best friends, and my husband now lives with a bona-fide dedicated "Bible Thumper" as he likes to call me, but again, I would not have it any other way. What a blessing to have been chosen by God. To be counted as one of His children!

I encourage you to check and make sure you are in the faith. Work out your sanctification with fear and trembling. Do a fruit's audit. There are several tools in the back of this book that may help you. I want you to have that blessed assurance that Jesus is in fact yours, and you are His! My prayer is that you will start with your faith, then dig into the purpose and promises God has for you and your future. Prayerfully read through this book and mark it up as you go along. Re-read chapters that you find difficult or somehow go against your instincts. Dig deeper into scripture. Test what I share by looking at what the Bible says, rather than basing things on your feelings. Pray that God would abundantly fill you with the Holy Spirit as He teaches you His word!

PART 1

DOMESTICATING GOD

CHAPTER 1

THE DOMESTICATED GOD

"God said to Moses, "I AM WHO I AM."
And he said, "Say this to the people of Israel:
'I AM has sent me to you.'"
Exodus 3:14 ESV

The word domesticate means to make the thing that doesn't fit, fit. Like the domesticated dog, we have successfully trained them to do their business in certain places, walk by our side, heel, sit, and come on command. We want them to live by our rules. When a person attempts to domesticate God, they do the same things. In my case, I was picking and choosing from the Bible what I decided worked for me and threw out the rest as antiquated. I remember a time in my life when I only prayed to God when it was convenient, namely, when I needed something that would serve me and my desires.

Domesticating God is when a person chooses to force God's will to align with theirs. For me, I took my feelings about what I thought was right and wrong, and made sweeping assumptions that God's will was the same as mine. I took God and put Him in a box that neatly fit my standards. The sad reality is, we all have done it, each and every one of us!

How, then, do we un-domesticate God?
The simple answer is to raise our view of God.

Our historically low view of God is what got us into this mess of domesticating God in the first place. A. W. Tozer (1897-1963) states, "What comes into our minds when we think about God is the most important thing about us." This statement may be a lot to unpack, but once understood, may be one of the most profoundly true statements about man's relationship to God. C.S. Lewis argued the opposite by stating, "How God thinks of us is not only more important, but infinitely more important." Lewis considered that question is the more important of the two. Man's relationship to God, while important to us as humans, is not really that important at all.

"Does the clay say to him who forms it, 'What are you making?'" (Isaiah 45:9 ESV)

While Tozer's quote regarding what comes into our minds when we think about God may be helpful in revealing a person's heart, it is God's purpose that is most important.

Let me ask you, "What comes to your mind when you think about God?" Take a moment to think about that. Does your mind conjure up a big Grandpa figure in the sky that upon meeting, you will curl up in his eternally warm, soft, and peaceful lap? Is God like the father you never had? Someone you can trust and be there when you need Him to be? Is God someone who set the world in motion, showed up a few times in ancient history, then left us all to fend for ourselves?

Allow me to pose a slightly different question, "What do you think it will be like when you meet God for the first time face to face?" Will you give Him a joyous enraptured embrace like so many artists' portrayals of heaven depict? Will you shake the hand of Jesus and offer your respectful thanks? Will you rattle off the thousands of unanswered questions you have stored away in your mind about the world?

The reality of when you encounter God face to face, for the first time, will most likely be so very different from what you believe it will be. I imagine I will be floored, literally. Of the several times in the Bible where we read when people realize they are standing in front of a holy God, their responses are often similar: they feel utterly ashamed, ruined, and unworthy. When you meet God for the first time, it will be a holy encounter for sure. I'm guessing, based on what the Bible teaches, that the holiness of the one true God will be so overwhelming that all I will be able to do is get as flat as I possibly can, be as quiet as I can, in total and complete submission to Him.

The third question I would like to ask you to think about is, "What do you think comes to God's mind when He thinks about you?" With a head bowed low, I consider this question to have the most impact on my actions. Of course we all want to hear, *"Well done, my good and faithful servant."* (Matthew 25:21 ESV) When faced with the question of what comes to God's mind when He thinks of me, even though I long to hear Him say "well done," I also deeply feel the weight of my sin. I have had my heart crushed and rebuilt through the power of the Holy Spirit, and I know all too well that *"all our righteous deeds are like a polluted garment"* (Isaiah 64:6 ESV) and *"None is righteous, no, not one;"* (Romans 3:10 ESV). It is only through the blood of Jesus that I will hear those beautiful words from God!

C.S. Lewis put it best when he wrote,
"To please God... to be a real ingredient in the divine happiness... to be loved by God, not merely pitied, but

delighted in as an artist delights in his work or a father in a son—it seems impossible, a weight or burden of glory which our thoughts can hardly sustain. But so it is."

It boggles my mind that God delights in me. I have confidence in this wondrous fact. The goal, then, is to let God be God and raise my view of God so high that when I see Him on that Day, I will know for certain He will call me by name because of Jesus. Through all of my mistakes and weaknesses, He still delights in me as I try to do the best I can to help build His kingdom and bring Him glory.

The reality is there are dangerous distractions in our world that push against our view of God. Satan knows that lowering our view of Him, even those who are saved, will go a long way in helping him and his minions to deceive us. The great lies the devil tells us are sweet like the fruit of Eden, dripping with goodness and genuine love for others. There are lies that may be taught in our churches, by our family and friends, and even through our potentially deceptive logical thought process. Our own heart is the most dangerous culprit of all and the devil knows this. He twists and distorts our view of salvation so that, to the world, it looks like Christianity, but in reality is something vastly different.

My heart aches even thinking about this because I was one who bought the devil's lies hook, line, and sinker. For 22 years I believed I was saved because I believed I had the right to choose how I felt about God, and live based on my *feelings* rather than His word. I was even someone who read the Bible; I read and studied all of the time. I was the person my friends came to when they had a question about the Bible. My mind thought it was right, and my heart emotionally followed close behind. I allowed Satan's worldly distractions to cloak the truth.

I did not write this book for any other reason than to help people see Jesus more clearly. I wrote it for the person who has a tug at their heart to forget what other people are telling them about God, and hear the hard truths of what God wants to tell them about who He is.

I want to support you in this journey and help you get one step closer to Jesus. I pray that your walk with God becomes stronger and more filled with the Holy Spirit. I pray that God would bless you with overflowing spiritual wisdom. I pray that you would be protected from evil and that you would not be deceived. Are these the things you pray for yourself and friends too?

CHAPTER 2

THE ART OF DECEPTION

*"For false christs and false prophets will arise
and perform signs and wonders,
to lead astray, if possible, the elect."*
Mark 13:22 ESV

Deception is meant to fool you into thinking something is really true, when it is not. One way that we knowingly delight in being deceived is with a magician. Even today, people who are called mentalists, psychics, or mediums sometimes trick people into really thinking there is truth to the deception. A couple of tricks and all of a sudden the thing that is fake looks and seems real. As cynical as our nation is, it sure is good at thinking things are true when they aren't.

How often have you read a title of a news article that used a scandalous headline to draw people in, and based solely on the title, you came to a conclusion about the story? Deception is real. It is all around us. It is meant to fool us. The reality of deception, though, is not in the trickery or the click-bait hype that marketers want you to fall for. The real issue with deception is that the most believable deceivers are those who passionately believe what they are saying is, in fact, true!

Deception is seen in "name-it-and-claim-it" theology, "easy-believism," and the "prosperity gospel." Those spreading deception do not feel they are the deceivers. They feel *you* are being deceived and they are saving you from yourself! So how do you spot deception? How do you know if you are being deceived? How do you know if you are the one deceiving others? Who God is has nothing to do with how you feel. Gravity has nothing to do with your feelings. It is true truth. Here, on this planet, gravity is real, even if you do not believe in it. Physical truths are easier to understand than spiritual ones, however there is a very real way to determine what is true and what is not, even in the spiritual realm.

When it comes to who God is, you must first decide if you believe in God. Take a quick look at your hand or a rose and you will start to understand what the Grand Design is. Scientists have tried endlessly to create artificial intelligence that matches a human. No man has even come close to replicating what God has done with the intricacies of a tiny ant, or a human being, or even all the way up to the intricacies of our vast and complicated universe.

Satan understands this is war. His goal is not to get droves of people who are already dead to stay dead. His goal is to get droves and droves of people who are seeking answers, seeking truth, and seeking Christ, to be deceived. Let's look at a few verses:

"But false prophets also arose among the people, just as there will be false teachers among you, who will secretly bring in destructive heresies, even denying the Master who bought them, bringing upon themselves swift destruction. And many will follow their sensuality, and because of them the way of truth will be blasphemed. And in their greed they will exploit you with false words. Their condemnation from long ago is not idle, and their destruction is not asleep." (2 Peter 2:1-3 ESV)

"For such men are false apostles, deceitful workmen, disguising themselves as apostles of Christ. And no wonder, for even Satan disguises himself as an angel of light. So it is no surprise

if his servants, also, disguise themselves as servants of righteousness. Their end will correspond to their deeds."
(2 Corinthians 11:13-15 ESV)

"For false christs and false prophets will arise and perform signs and wonders, to lead astray, if possible, the elect."
(Mark 13:22 ESV)

How do you know for sure if you are one of the deceived or one who is deceiving others? The simple answer is to know what the Bible teaches as a whole, not piecemeal. There may be well-intentioned people in your life who are steeped in heresy. Heresy is having an opinion or belief that is contrary to orthodox views of Christianity. Orthodox means what is traditionally agreed upon as true based on the Bible.

Heresy is continually on the rise across America as we see everything from political giants to box-office hits twist Biblical truths. Mainstream media, and some pastors, such as Joel Osteen and Benny Hinn, show us how easy it is to create a "feel good" gospel that is centered around self-gratification and self-glorification rather than Christ. Man-centered theology is an oxymoron and should not be tolerated by any Christian.

We must diligently watch out for heresy in our church and in ourselves too. In Galatians 1:8-9 (ESV), Paul was making his condemnation doubly clear, when he states basically the same sentence twice.

"But even if we or an angel from heaven should preach to you a gospel contrary to the one we preached to you, let him be accursed. As we have said before, so now I say again: If anyone is preaching to you a gospel contrary to the one you received, let him be accursed." (Galatians 1:8-9 ESV)

By stating the same thing, back-to-back, two times, he is, in effect, giving them a harsher condemnation. He was making certain that the Galatians knew it was wrong to preach anything contrary to the true gospel. His repetition also implies that having false pastors (preachers and teachers) in our church is something that could and would happen often and possibly without notice. Heresy seeps in so insidiously.

It may be hard to decipher if we are under sound preaching. We assume our pastor went to seminary and was taught only Biblical truths. We assume, and rightfully so, that they should know more than us, and that they have our best interest at heart. However, a look at the path the American mainstream church has taken, we ought to think twice and take another look at our own church. We must be good "Bereans," or students, and do the work ourselves.

But how would we know if we have placed ourselves under a pastor who is unknowingly teaching a false gospel? Sadly, many do not. They just go to church and Bible study and let others tell them what they should believe. We assume that verses such as Acts 20:29-30 couldn't apply to our pastor. This is why deception is so subtle and harmful.

"I know that after my departure fierce wolves will come in among you, not sparing the flock; and from among your own selves will arise men speaking twisted things, to draw away the disciples after them." (Acts 20:29-30 ESV)

Deception creeps its way in through self-centered behavior that comes with human power. Man craves it, and it is one of the easiest ways Satan gets into the heart of man (even Christians, and possibly even a pastor). Think about it...

does your pastor teach directly from the Bible or does he teach topically on everyday issues then throws a verse or two in? Is there a way you can tell if what he is teaching is man-centered or God-centered?

It may be helpful to ask yourself a few questions. When you go to church are you interested in what the pastor has to say? Do you like what he is preaching? Do you feel good after the message? Did he give you sound advice on how to be a better person in society? Or do you leave feeling convicted with a desire to spread the gospel to others and sacrifice your comforts for the good of the Cross? In mainstream religion, one gets the sense that people want to hear from teachers about things they need help with to feel good.

"For the time is coming when people will not endure sound teaching, but having itching ears they will accumulate for themselves teachers to suit their own passions"
(2 Timothy 4:3 ESV)

Men (and now many women) behind pulpits will rise up, preaching with passion using the Bible as their cloak. They will say, "Listen to me, read my books, and do my studies, and you will be considered a good Christian." Has your church turned into a self-help program? Many have.

The mega-churches, or rather, monster-churches of today can be frightening. There are a ton of mega-churches out there, but it's not difficult to imagine that many may be under false teaching. You can tell what they are about by the conviction they teach and by the fruits of the congregation. A God-centered message is full of conviction, not ear tickling, and the congregation will bear good fruit. The alternative will bear no fruit at all, even possibly wickedness in the case of my first church where all of the main pastors were involved in various scandals, one after the other, from the top down.

Consider Jesus' own ministry. Jesus did not say, "Come, hang out, I've got a playground for the kids, and we will be doing a carnival for the family with lots of free food and fun activities that will make you feel like a good person, oh, and by the way, follow me, it's awesome, I love you and have a wonderful plan for your life." Nope, I still can't find any of that in the Bible.

Jesus said things like, be overjoyed when you are persecuted on His account, and when someone hits you on the face, turn and allow him to hit your other cheek, and how about loving your enemies, or that all other religions are false (no tolerance from Jesus on this one), or that your pursuit of money is a pursuit against God.

The mark of a good pastor is, in large part, teaching the truths Jesus taught even if such sermons might just cause people to leave. Jesus' ministry had MANY people leaving from teachings that were too hard to hear. Some pastors and elder boards may get too hung up on keeping their organization's financial books out of the red, filling the pews, having more "amens" during the sermon, and more pats on the back from their parishioners afterwards. Here are a couple of things Jesus said that were very hard to understand or do.

> *"If anyone comes to me and does not hate his own father and mother and wife and children and brothers and sisters, yes, even his own life, he cannot be my disciple."* (Luke 14:26 ESV)

"Truly, truly, I say to you, unless you eat the flesh of the Son of Man and drink his blood, you have no life in you." (John 6:53 ESV)

John 6:60 (ESV) states *"When many of his disciples heard it, they said, "This is a hard saying; who can listen to it?"* Did you catch that? It said many, not some. And again in verse 66 of John 6 it says, *"After this many* (again MANY, not some) *of his disciples* (not just random people listening but His DISCIPLES) *turned back and no longer walked with him."* {!!!!}

This should knock the breath out of you! They turned back! They no longer followed Him! Wow! Do you understand now? Take a good hard look at who you are placing your soul under to teach you about God's Truth. They are just men. Not only do you need to make sure you trust your pastor and make sure you find a good one who is, above all else, humble to the Holy Spirit's guidance, but you must also become a student of God's word. Not a student of commentaries, but a student of the Bible. Read it. More now than you ever have before. It is *that* important! Following Jesus means living a life of identifying and rooting out deception wherever you find it.

CHAPTER 3

PROOF OF LIFE

"Examine yourselves, to see whether you are in the faith."
2 Corinthians 13:5 ESV

There is this self-justifying internal response that happens to many of us when we think about being good or bad. You may try to tell yourself you are okay; you are better than most people, right? You may say to yourself, "God loves me. Of course I am going to heaven." You may be assuming your own salvation to the potential life-ending detriment of your soul. Paul tells us in his second letter to the Corinthians, *"Examine yourselves, to see whether you are in the faith."* (2 Corinthians 13:5 ESV) It is okay to examine yourself!

When you were born, your parents were very aware of your growth. They had 100% proof that you were growing. If you were not, you would be taken immediately to the doctor. I remember having my baby and freaking out because his weight was in the 10th percentile. I was searching for any cause of lack of weight gain. When he was a toddler I obsessed over the fact that his feet seemed to not be growing at all, while the other kids in his class had shoe sizes that were three sizes bigger.

Moms search for evidence and want constant evidence of growth. How is it then, that it is not a common thing in Christian circles to question one's faith or to even search for proof of growth? To have assurance in your own salvation is a huge thing. The word "hope," in biblical terms, does not just mean you hope it might come true one day. It actually means "confident assurance." That is a very different meaning, and I think you would love to have confident assurance in the fact that you are going to heaven, am I correct?

Don't let another moment go by without checking to see if you are, indeed, saved. On October 8, 1871, American evangelist, D.L. Moody, gave a sermon to his massive congregation where he ended the sermon by asking them to go home and consider their salvation and perhaps come back next week with a decision for Christ. On that night the Great Chicago Fire swept through the city burning his church to the ground, killing almost 300 people, and leaving over 100,000 people homeless. He vowed to never ask people to sit on their decision again. The gospel message is always urgent, and while it was not Moody's job to save anyone, he knew, from that moment on, that it was important to make sure his congregation understood that salvation was something not to be taken lightly.

Is your view of God skewed to the point of being confused about what you believe? Is there a sense of uneasiness surrounding your salvation? Do you tell yourself that it is only the devil that is causing you to doubt? Did you know that doubt is normal, yet there is a way to know 100%, with absolute certainty, that you are saved? Many choose to not even think about it because it is too scary or difficult to approach this subject. Let's consider some areas we may have domesticated God that may not be fun to discuss. Before you move forward, please stop and pray to God. Ask Him to reveal Himself to you and to give you peace, clarity, and a teachable spirit.

CHAPTER 4

TICKET TO HEAVEN

*"Repent therefore, and turn back,
that your sins may be blotted out."*
Acts 3:19 ESV

The domestication of God can be seen clearly in the widely popular view of Universalism or Universal Reconciliation. People want to believe that salvation is for everyone, meaning every person will eventually go to heaven. The Bible clearly doesn't teach this. People also want to believe that if you say a magic prayer, that man has termed "The Sinner's Prayer" (which, by the way, is not in the Bible), then they are saved and have their ticket to heaven. While I understand the motives behind the idea of this prayer as wanting to be helpful, I fear too many people now put too much weight on it. They may mistakenly think that this prayer contains the words one must utter to be saved. Conversion is a posture of the heart, not mere words.

People want to believe it is their choice to be "born again," and anyone can be saved as long as they call on the Lord. (Romans 10:13) Declaring "Jesus is Lord" is all you have to do to be saved. (Romans 10:9) *"Even the demons believe—and shudder!"* (James 2:19 ESV) So, does this mean demons can be saved? By no means! They made their choice and their judgment is final, but with us there is hope!

39

When it comes to human free will and choosing God, let me share three parables.

The first parable takes us on a trip in an airplane. Our human free will is part of our dignity. God created us in His image with the ability to reason, discern, laugh, love, and judge as part of our human uniqueness. Free will is often confused with the ability for a person to choose to be saved. Consider taking a trip to another country. Your final destination is already determined. You board the plane. You have dignity and free will to order chips or a soda, stand up and walk the aisle during the flight, take a nap, watch a movie, or any other "free will" choices. What you cannot change is your final destination, as it has already been predetermined, ahead of time.

The second parable is about a thief and a murderer. Jane is a good person, who loves people. A bad man comes into her home, rapes her daughter, murders her son, takes all of her valuable possessions, and then trashes her home. A while later, he comes back to Jane and demands that she bend the knee and offers her hand in marriage to him. How do you think Jane should respond? Consider this in light of God. How is it that someone who is an enemy of God, can tell God to save them? Did we not sin against Him and murder His Son?

How low a view of God to think that we, as enemies of God, have any say in our salvation! How low a view of God to think that we, as sinners dead in our transgressions, can become alive at our choosing. Did you tell your mom that you were ready to be conceived and born into this world? Let me share one more story with you.

The third parable is about our pet rabbit. We live in an area that is infested with rabbits. They destroy our garden and make a mess of pretty much everything. One day my son asked me, "Mom, can I have a pet bunny?" Being the economical person that I am, I set a trap in the yard. Sure enough I caught one. It was clean enough, so I took it to the vet to have it checked out, thoroughly cleaned, and to get all of its shots. I wouldn't want to bring it into the house full of disease, now would I? I went to the pet store, bought a cute little cage house with all of the bells and whistles, and brought our new pet bunny rabbit home to my child, much to his excitement.

The bunny was given a new name, Button. Button the Bunny was loved, played with, fed the best food, and slept on the softest bedding. Meanwhile, out in the back yard, a rebellion was forming. The other rabbits were quite upset. They were grumbling amongst themselves and questioning why Button, formerly known as Brutus, was getting all of the attention. Why did he get to sleep inside? Why was he always fat and happy? Why him and not them?

Do you often ask why some people are saved and others are not? Why would God condemn a "good person" to hell just because he or she is not chosen? How/why does God choose in the first place?! It is possibly one of the most difficult theological dilemmas humans face. This could be an example of domesticating God, one that may have some hidden ramifications. The doctrine of election doesn't seem to fit with our get-what-you-earn idea of salvation. It cuts to the core of our desire for all of our loved ones to be saved. Why would God choose some over others? What if your spouse or children are not among those who are chosen? You may be tempted to say, "How dare God do that to me?" This dilemma isn't particularly new. In fact, it's another way to frame the Problem of Evil. How can a good God allow for bad things to happen? More on this in Chapter 8.

Consider this: it is not about why some are going to heaven and some are going to hell. The real question is "Why are *any* of us going to heaven?" Do any of us deserve heaven? The answer is, "No! None of us deserve anything!" In the case of Button the Bunny, it was not about why he was chosen and none of the rest were, it was about why *any* of the rabbits were chosen at *all*. I am in charge of my own backyard, and if I choose to help a bunny, then so be it. If I choose, I can get an exterminator and eliminate them all like in the days of Noah. (Genesis 7:4 and Matthew 24:38-39)

To ask an even harder question, "Why would someone be created by God as a vessel of wrath?" One of the hardest passages in the Bible to reconcile as a human is found in Romans 9. Pastors may avoid this passage in sermons because it's rather difficult to unpack the context of Paul's words in light of his overarching argument in Romans. They may save this for more in-depth Bible studies outside of the general Sunday service, or perhaps, not cover it at all.

> *"But who are you, O man, to answer back to God? Will what is molded say to its molder, "Why have you made me like this?" Has the potter no right over the clay, to make out of the same lump one vessel for honorable use and another for dishonorable use? What if God, desiring to show his wrath and to make known his power, has endured with much patience vessels of wrath prepared for destruction, in order to make known the riches of his glory for vessels of mercy, which he has prepared beforehand for glory— even us whom he has called, not from the Jews only but also from the Gentiles?"* (Romans 9:20-24 ESV)

Think about the life and death of Judas, the one who betrayed Jesus. He was necessary to fulfill God's plan. Jesus even said it would have been better for Judas if he was never born. We see in scripture many people created as a vessel of wrath. Judas might have thought it was not fair, but we know that, in the end, everyone will accept their fate. Every knee will bow. Everyone will confess verbally that Jesus is Lord.

"Therefore God has highly exalted him and bestowed on him the name that is above every name, so that at the name of Jesus every knee should bow, in heaven and on earth and under the earth, and every tongue confess that Jesus Christ is Lord, to the glory of God the Father." (Philippians 2:9-11 ESV)

If no one deserves salvation, and we don't ultimately have a say in what type of vessel we were created to be, then how can we be sure we are saved and how can we even be saved in the first place? It all sounds so tragic, but there is hope! Your salvation is something that is between you and God. Let's dive into a deeper understanding of who God is and how He works based on what the Bible tells us. I am prayerful that you may gain clarity on this through the Holy Spirit!

CHAPTER 5

GOD'S SOVEREIGNTY

"I know that you can do all things,
and that no purpose of yours can be thwarted."
Job 42:2 ESV

Do you believe God is sovereign; that He created everything and has control over everything? R.C. Sproul put it this way about God's sovereignty,

> "Everything that happens must at least happen by his permission. If he permits something, then he must decide to allow it. If he decides to allow something, then in a sense he is foreordaining it. Who, among Christians, would argue that God could not stop something in this world from happening? If God so desires, he has the power to stop the whole world. To say that God foreordains all that comes to pass is simply to say that God is sovereign over his entire creation. If something could come to pass apart from his sovereign permission, then that which came to pass would frustrate his sovereignty. If God refused to permit something to happen and it happened anyway, then whatever caused it to happen would have more authority and power than God himself. If there is any part of creation outside of Gods sovereignty, then God is simply not sovereign. If God is not sovereign, then God is not God." – R.C. Sproul "Chosen by God"

If God is sovereign, fully in control of every molecule, then we must loosen our grip on how we feel He should be running things. Raise your view of God, and give over the controls.

The point of this is not to cause you to doubt or to cause you to be angry with a view of God you do not like. The point is to help you see the reality of your own standing in front of a holy God. Undomesticate God a little bit further by trusting that your simple desire to read a book that challenges you, is evidence of the grand and mighty work of the sovereignty of God and the Holy Spirit in your life drawing you to Jesus in an inexplicable, yet irresistible way.

Because God is in control of every molecule, He is the one who ultimately makes salvation and the work of the Holy Spirit irresistible. If we examine the Scripture and hold it up against salvation stories of Christians throughout history past and present, one thing is glaringly true in all accounts: the work of the Holy Spirit before conversion. If you are wondering right now, if you are one who is chosen and saved, then consider the work of the Holy Spirit in your own life.

The passage in John 16 regarding the work of the Holy Spirit is a good place to start when trying to understand the spark that ignites conversion.

> *"Nevertheless, I tell you the truth: it is to your advantage that I go away, for if I do not go away, the Helper will not come to you. But if I go, I will send him to you. And when he comes, he will convict the world concerning sin and righteousness and judgment: concerning sin, because they do not believe in me; concerning righteousness, because I go to the Father, and*

you will see me no longer; concerning judgment, because the ruler of this world is judged. "I still have many things to say to you, but you cannot bear them now. When the Spirit of truth comes, he will guide you into all the truth, for he will not speak on his own authority, but whatever he hears he will speak, and he will declare to you the things that are to come. He will glorify me, for he will take what is mine and declare it to you. All that the Father has is mine; therefore I said that he will take what is mine and declare it to you."
(John 16:7-14 ESV)

There are three main areas listed in John 16:8 to take note of regarding what the Helper's job is. The Helper is another name for the Holy Spirit. To help understand this passage, I worked through it with a trusted pastor, and also consulted the Strong's Concordance to determine the meaning of the word "convict." In the ESV the Greek word for convict is "elegchō." Elegchō means to convict, convince, and reprove (reprimand). For the purposes of understanding this verse more clearly, I will use those three words.

"And when he comes, he will convict the world concerning sin and righteousness and judgment:" (John 16:8 ESV)

1. Sin – The Holy Spirit will convince, convict, and reprove the person of their need to trust and submit to Christ.

2. Righteousness – The Holy Spirit will convince, convict, and reprove the person that they fall short of the perfect standard God has placed before them, and therefore, they need Christ as their proxy.

3. Judgment – The Holy Spirit will convince, convict, and reprove the person that rebellion is a charge against God that will be punished. They should repent and cease their rebellion against God.

With a clear understanding of Holy Spirit's role in light of God's sovereignty, it is important to consider the role of sin and how the Holy Spirit works in the individual before, during, and after conversion.

CHAPTER 6

THE HOLY SPIRIT AT WORK

"And when he comes, he will convict the world
concerning sin and righteousness and judgment:"
John 16:8 ESV

"My appeal is addressed to those who have been previously taught in secret by the wisdom of God. I speak to thirsty hearts whose longings have been wakened by the touch of God within them, and such as they need no reasoned proof. Their restless hearts furnish all the proof they need." – A.W. Tozer, *The Pursuit of God*

Do you feel the weight of your sin? When I have conversations with non-Christian people about sin, most do not think they are really that bad of a sinner. Most would say they aren't a sinner at all. They may choose to define their sin as shortcomings, weaknesses, maybe even failures, but not sin. I even see this response from some in Christian circles too. They claim they do not murder or steal. They claim white lies aren't really lies. Sins are relative. Everyone cheats on their taxes so that is not really lying or stealing, right?

What separates Christianity from every other religion on the planet is the way Jesus described sin. All religions, and even moral people who consider themselves to be non-religious, typically all agree when it comes to the big sins. They agree that murder is wrong, stealing is wrong, lying is wrong, sleeping with a married person is wrong, along with many other rules that help our society not completely fall apart in anarchy. This is called natural law. Some might describe it as moralism, which is based on human effort. Jesus, on the other hand, took it all to a completely different level. This is what Jesus says in about murder,

"You have heard that it was said to those of old, 'You shall not murder; and whoever murders will be liable to judgment.' But I say to you that everyone who is angry with his brother will be liable to judgment; whoever insults his brother will be liable to the council; and whoever says, 'You fool!' will be liable to the hell of fire." (Matthew 5:21-22 ESV)

What Jesus just said is very different than simple moralism. Here we see what His views are on adultery,

"You have heard that it was said, 'You shall not commit adultery.' But I say to you that everyone who looks at a woman with lustful intent has already committed adultery with her in his heart." (Matthew 5:27-28 ESV)

Are we all doomed?

When my child does something wrong, he instinctively tries to hide it or cover it up. Remember Adam and Eve in the garden trying to hide from God after they disobeyed Him? (Genesis 3:8-11) We all understand this type of human guilt. My son has justified many of his wrongdoings as totally acceptable on the sheer premise that he was not caught. Human guilt can only get us so far, because our sin nature will try to cover it up and then justify it so we are not overcome with guilt. While yes, we all have a sinful nature, sin can also be used to describe the very core of our nature. Sinful acts are the outpouring of our sin nature. This is why I use the term "sin nature" rather than sinful nature.

The Holy Spirit, on the other hand, works in a way that is inescapable. When you feel the Holy Spirit start to convince and convict you of your sin, you will start to understand the major difference between human guilt and spiritual guilt. Spiritual guilt, spurred on by the Holy Spirit, is when your guilt consumes you to the point of repentance admitting fault. Guilt consumes you to the point of a necessary confession to the one you wronged, be it another person, yourself, or God. There is no escaping your fault, no hiding it, and no justifying it. There is only confession and repentance.

If the Holy Spirit is inside you, meaning you are truly saved, it will be extremely hard to sin, and *not* desire to make things right. Christians sin all of the time, this side of heaven. That is just a fact. The question is how do you respond to that sin? There is no timing on your repentance, as it may take a minute, a day, or even a week to make it right. If you are truly a Christian, and you have let something you have done wrong go beyond a normal amount of time, you will agree that it will be a burden. There will be a continual nagging at your soul until you finally confess and repent.

There is no formula to this, but the simple act of spiritual conviction is noticeably different than human conviction. If you are saved, you understand the difference. If you feel like you do not experience the Holy Spirit's conviction, then going back to the basics of the gospel message is an important thing to work out. If you are saved, you will delight in going through the gospel message again! Before we move into understanding the full Gospel message, it is important that we set the foundation first. We must start with understanding where we get this gospel message from: the Bible. Can you be sure that the Bible is the Truth with a capital "T"?

CHAPTER 7

THE BIBLE

"But be doers of the word,
and not hearers only, deceiving yourselves."
James 1:22 ESV

If you believe in God, then the next step is to understand what God's plan is. You can find this in the Bible. Many religious people-groups have tried to discredit the Bible. They come up with their own doctrines. They may even claim the Bible has been distorted and changed. Again, if you do the research, you will find that the Bible is the most verified book of any book on the planet throughout history.

This book you are reading now is not a book on the veracity of the Bible. There have been too many historians and scholars prove the Bible is verified historically and the accounts in the Bible actually happened. Jesus *did* exist, He historically *did* the things we are told about in the Bible with all of the miracles and healings, He actually *was* nailed to a cross, He biologically died and was buried for three days, and He rose again (came back to life). He was then seen by over 500 eyewitnesses. Jesus is utterly unique in these regards.

If you want to read a good book to help you understand the veracity of the Bible, I suggest "Case for Christ" by Lee Strobel. Read the book rather than watch the movie, which does not do the book justice, in my opinion.

If you believe in God, and you believe that the Bible is God's word, then you can figure out if you are being deceived or are deceiving others. Believe me when I say, I never want to deceive others. It is something my entire career is dedicated to. I work in an industry that is steeped in deception and lies. My goal has always been to shed light on the truth both in my work and when it comes to God.

Do you know how easy it is to make the Bible say what you want it to? People (and even some pastors) do this often; they take verses out of context to spread their personal message. Many believers struggle with this temptation, myself included. We pick and choose individual Bible verses and take them out of context to help prove our point, rather than desiring to see God's point. How can we stop doing this? By studying the Bible. There are two main methods of studying and teaching the Bible: deductive and inductive. It is important to distinguish between these two forms of Bible study.

Deductive Bible study is considering a topic and then finding individual Bible verses to help support that topic. This, in my opinion, is a potentially dangerous way of study and teaching. A clear example would be when someone takes a Bible verse like Philippians 4:13 (ESV) and twists the original meaning to make it fit with the topic. *"I can do all things through him who strengthens me."* I have seen this verse specifically in a well-known pastor's Christian weight-loss study. This verse had nothing to do with human goals like weight-loss. The specific sentence in the letter to the Philippians was written by Paul to Timothy to let him know that even in chains Paul could be content in all things. By the intended context, you should be content if you are overweight. Please go ahead and read all of Philippians 4 and look at the full context of this verse.

Another example of this is seen in John 10:10 (ESV), *"The thief comes only to steal and kill and destroy. I came that they may have life and have it abundantly."* If you read this verse based on the modern usage of words, you might be inclined to think Jesus came to give you an abundant life now, in this lifetime. If you read it in the original context, with an understanding of the original meaning of the Greek word "perissos" that is translated as "abundant" as it pertains to life, you will find that Jesus is referring to eternal life. It has the implications of "beyond," or in this case, the afterlife. Jesus wants you to have eternal life, not more riches and happiness here in this life.

One may be inclined to defend this type of Bible reading by giving the verse that says the Word of God is living and active. One might even argue that allowing a verse to minister to them, even if that is not what it meant in the original context, is what God wants.

> *"For the word of God is living and active, sharper than any two-edged sword, piercing to the division of soul and of spirit, of joints and of marrow, and discerning the thoughts and intentions of the heart."* (Hebrews 4:12 ESV)

The original context of Hebrews 4:12 is about the Word of God having the ability to *save souls* and help guide us, not allow us to use it in any way that makes us feel good. As an author this can be very scary. One of the main things I write about is health and wellness through the use of essential oils. I often refer to the essential oils in my books as simply oil. What if a mechanic read a sentence in my book that said, "It can be very healthful for you to consume up to 12 drops of oil per day"? If that mechanic started to put automotive oil in his or her coffee each morning, they might end up in the hospital. Context is so very important and as a child of the One who wrote the Bible, I am extremely protective of His Word! This is why I encourage you to use the inductive study method.

Inductive study is a way of taking specific verses and making sense of them based on the context and broader message as seen throughout the entire Bible. It is observing the context of the who, what, where, when, and how, then interpreting that to what it means in a universal sense, and then applying it to your personal life now.

This is why expository preaching is also so important. Find a pastor that teaches the whole Bible. One who takes the book chapter by chapter. They will not be able to skip over hard verses, and they will not be able to make a verse mean what they want it to say.

To take someone's writing completely out of context is not helpful and is disrespectful to the author. It only harms the complete message. The first and best thing you can do to guard yourself against deception is to check it out. Go ahead and look things up. Bring your Bible to church. Read it... read it often! Don't just go to the books you like. Read the whole thing! Pray that God would give you a desire to read His Word. Find friends who want to read along with you in a daily Bible reading plan so that you can enjoy the experience together. Be intentional about talking about what you read each day. I do this with my friends online and find it to be both rewarding and helpful in keeping me on track, but also to ask questions and get help when I need it.

CHAPTER 8

THE QUESTION OF EVIL

"For God is not a God of confusion but of peace."
1 Corinthians 14:33 ESV

Without the Bible, we run the risk of making assumptions about God: who He is, what His character is, and what His plan of salvation looks like. We domesticate God by stealing his identity from Him through our self-derived ideals and thoughts about who we *think* He should be.

Jay Adams states in his book, *The Grand Demonstration,*
"Speculation about the ways of God that He has not revealed to us is wrong. To do it is attempted robbery. If, as He says, unrevealed truths about Himself and His purposes "belong" to Him, and not to us, the attempt to pry those secrets from His hand by means of human reasoning is nothing less than attempted theft."

The issue here is that we may be making God into something He is not. He has given us the Bible. It's how He's chosen to reveal Himself. However, to assume God has revealed everything about who He is in the Bible would be naive. Alternatively, to assume something about Him that He has *not* revealed would be blasphemy. Don't do it! A.W. Tozer categorized this activity of making God into something He is not as a major sin of idolatry.

"Among the sins to which the human heart is prone, hardly any other is more hateful to God than idolatry, for idolatry is at bottom a libel on His character. The idolatrous heart assumes that God is other than He is — in itself a monstrous sin — and substitutes for the true God one made after its own likeness. Always this God will conform to the image of the one who created it and will be base or pure, cruel or kind, according to the moral state of the mind from which it emerges." – A.W. Tozer, *The Knowledge of the Holy*

One area that seems hard for some people to deal with or find peace in, is confronting the theological debate surrounding the "Problem of Evil." Why do bad things happen to good people? If God is so good, then why does He allow innocent babies to die at birth, or worse, get murdered, or why are there wars, and disease, and terrible things that happen to those who do not deserve it? Why does He allow calamity to befall on His children?

God is not the source of evil. While He created all things, He did not create evil. One way to understand this is through the imagery of light and dark. The light does not create the dark. Where there is darkness, that just means it is void of light. While God may allow evil to happen, He is not the creator of it, nor is He the one who inflicts evil on people. We live in a fallen world based on our choices. He may create vessels of wrath, but notice that He does not fill someone with evil wrath. He has righteous wrath, but when it comes to human unrighteous evil wrath, that is simply the absence of God.

"What if God, desiring to show his wrath and to make known his power, has endured with much patience vessels of wrath prepared for destruction," (Romans 9:22 ESV)

Another way to understand evil is to consider a world where there is only good. You would never truly understand good in the absence of evil. God doesn't need evil, but He is able to allow it to make known His power. Like a clear and perfect diamond shines brightest when placed on a black cloth, so does God's goodness shine brightest on the backdrop of evil and darkness allowing us to give Him glory all the more.

Where does this leave us? Why does God allow bad things to happen? Rather than pray for those bad things not to happen, perhaps a better response is to ask God what His will is in any given "bad" situation.

"And we know that for those who love God all things work together for good, for those who are called according to his purpose." (Romans 8:28 ESV)

Unpack Romans 8:28:

- We know (it is a fact)
- for those who love God (this is a promise for God's children, those who are saved)
- all things (this means ALL things, not some things)
- work together (everything is connected and on purpose)
- for good (good means GOD's good, not yours)
- for those who are called (again, those who are God's children, those who are saved. Note he says "called" which means God called you, you did not choose Him)
- according to His purpose (it is ALL about Him; not you and your needs)

Whenever a trial (test) or tribulation ("bad" thing) happens, I usually try to understand it from one of four angles. One of the best books written on this topic is by pastor and theologian, Dr. Mike Fabarez, called *Lifelines for Tough Times.* Dr. Fabarez states,

> "So if your current pain happens to be part of God's running process, it is understandable that you would be praying for it to go away. But as Jesus taught, this painful season is designed as part of God's perfect will for your life. It is not God's discipline to bring you to repent over some sinful decision. It is not the painful reaping from some foolish choices. It is not suffering that is associated with being a part of a fallen world. In this case, if it is the pruning of God, it is the loving and perfect will of God, and it will be used to make you a more productive Christian."

Dr. Fabarez sums up the four main areas that answer the question of why bad things happen.

1. God's pruning process in your life

2. God's discipline to bring you to repentance

3. Your own reaping of your foolish choices

4. Suffering that comes with being a part of a fallen world

The next time you are faced with a trial, tribulation, or confusingly awful situation, try to consider one of the above four reasons for why it may be happening to you. I have friends who have endured some of the most horrendous life experiences without any answers only to find out decades later why they were meant to go through that horrible thing.

Singer and songwriter, Laura Story, wrote a beautiful song called "Blessings" that helped me put into perspective the trials I face. The last part of the song says,

"When friends betray us – When darkness seems to win – We know that pain reminds this heart – That this is not our home – What if my greatest disappointments – Or the aching of this life – Is the revealing of a greater thirst this world can't satisfy – What if trials of this life – The rain, the storms, the hardest nights – Are your mercies in disguise."

While God does ask us to pray for everything (Philippians 4:6 and Hebrews 4:16), and He delights in us doing so, I hope we can remember to honor and bring glory to God more by undomesticating Him in this area and considering what He desires our prayers to focus on. God has reasons for everything and He will use it for His good purposes. When you pray, remember that it's helpful to preface everything as Jesus did when He was hours away from the cross, *"Father, if you are willing, remove this cup from me. Nevertheless, not my will, but yours, be done."* (Luke 22:42 ESV)

Here are some helpful verses surrounding prayer. See Chapter 18 on Prayer for a more helpful understanding.

"Do not be anxious about anything, but in everything by prayer and supplication with thanksgiving let your requests be made known to God." (Philippians 4:6 ESV)

"Let us then with confidence draw near to the throne of grace, that we may receive mercy and find grace to help in time of need." (Hebrews 4:16 ESV)

"And when you pray, you must not be like the hypocrites. For they love to stand and pray in the synagogues and at the street corners, that they may be seen by others. Truly, I say to you, they have received their reward. But when you pray, go into your room and shut the door and pray to your Father who is in secret. And your Father who sees in secret will reward you. "And when you pray, do not heap up empty phrases as the Gentiles do, for they think that they will be heard for their many words. Do not be like them, for your Father knows what you need before you ask him." (Matthew 6:5-8 ESV)

PART 2

GOOD NEWS

CHAPTER 9

THE GOSPEL MESSAGE

···

"For God so loved the world,
that he gave his only Son,
that whoever believes in him
should not perish but have eternal life."
John 3:16 ESV

The word "gospel" simply means "good news." God's good news is that He has a plan to redeem His people back to Him. There are two ways of looking at the gospel message: what it is not, and what it is.

What the gospel message is not:

Have you ever considered the difference between a Christian by tradition and a Christian by faith? Many people assume they are Christians. They identify with Christianity as their religion because they were brought up that way. Others assume their choice of salvation is set in stone because they were baptized as a child, or because their parents expected them to make a profession of faith at an early age.

While child conversions are possible, as I never want to put God in a box, they aren't typical and here are some reasons why I believe this. God does not mention any conversion stories of toddlers and many parents can testify that a young child claiming Christianity can easily turn into a teenager that is far from being a Holy Spirit-filled Christian. Very young children are often more concerned with pleasing their parents. I experienced this with my own son who made a confession of faith at age five, and he, now at age 12, agrees that he is not saved. His heart was never regenerated, and he never bore any fruit. His was a peer-pressure "conversion."

Parents want to believe their child is saved at a young age, and while possible, it is important to look for signs of fruit. This is true for any age. Children are very susceptible to the pressures from their parents, and it is important to make sure their understanding, calling, and decision were their own.

While in many cases child conversions tend to not bear fruit, there are exceptions, and I do know people who were saved at a very early age, but it is not typical. If you were one who was saved in your single digit years, I encourage you to take a look at your entire story. Was there a time in later years that you truly understood the gospel and felt a major conviction of the Holy Spirit, or do you remember your conversion in your youth, and know that your regeneration and true sanctification started when you were very young?

Here are a few areas that people may mistake for the gospel message of salvation.

- Being born into a Christian family (I've always thought I was a Christian)
- Easy-believism (once saved, you don't need to change)
- Your ticket to heaven (if you claim Jesus you won't go to hell)
- Saying the "Sinner's Prayer" (some sort of magic words that make you saved)
- Prosperity gospel (name-it-and-claim-it theology)

- Being baptized (well-meaning parents who baptize infants or even 13-year-olds who do what their parents expect by being baptized may not be saved as baptism alone does not save you)

- Doing all the right things because it is expected of you: Going to church, giving money to the church, praying, reading the Bible (this is how the Pharisees lived, by checking off the boxes)

Many of these claims may be made by some people who identify with Christianity as their religion. It is a true domestication of God and unfortunately they would be on the wrong side of salvation when the Day of Judgment comes. Being born into a Christian family and feeling like you were always a Christian falls into one of the greatest traps of Satan called easy-believism. It is the opposite of Lordship salvation.

Lordship salvation means once you are saved you are no longer your own. You have died to yourself. The old has gone and the new has come. You are what is considered "born again." Your heart of stone has been turned into a heart of flesh. Basically this mean you are a slave to the One who saved you. Your whole life should now be dedicated to following His rules and His will, rather than your own. See the next chapter for more on Lordship salvation versus easy-believism and why it is an important distinction to make.

What the gospel message is:

The true gospel message calls us to respond to God's mercy and grace by believing in God, turning from your sins, and turning to Jesus by following Him and His commands. Many people misunderstand the word "believe" when it comes to the gospel. Remember, the demons believe. They know that God exists and that Jesus is the Son of God. They even believe their destruction is imminent. It is not about belief. It is about belief *in*.

Consider a heart surgeon. He or she goes to school, spends years in training, and masters (hopefully) the art and technique of heart surgery. One day you meet a young man who claims he is a heart surgeon. You may believe him, but to believe *in* him would be when you or a loved one needs open heart surgery and you allow him to operate. You would be putting your trust in him. That is believing *in* someone verses believing someone.

The gospel message is clear and simple. Below is a basic outline so you can easily memorize it. In the following pages, after the outline, is a more detailed description of the gospel. As you read through it, consider re-writing it in your own words. Keep the same basic message, but always utilize Scripture. Many will use what is called the Romans Road that outlines the gospel using passages from the book of Romans.

The Basics of the Gospel Message

- God is the Creator of everything and everyone
- He is the Creator, so He has a right to us as His creatures
- God is holy
- He is set apart; clean and pure
- God created humanity to be holy too
- Adam and Eve sinned by desiring to be god of themselves

- Selfishness and pride entered into our hearts through this original sin and is why we now have a sin nature
- Humanity is no longer holy; no longer clean and pure
- This unholiness and sin separates us from God
- God is just; sinners deserve to be punished for this disobedience
- A price must be paid; reconciliation to God only happens when the price is paid
- God is loving; God loves us so much that He sent His only son Jesus to come down to be the sacrifice
- Jesus lived a perfect life, the life humans were supposed to live but didn't, and died an undeserved death, the death we deserved but mercifully will not have to endure if we believe in Jesus
- Jesus paid the final price and then rose from the dead
- The Holy Spirit will convict His children of their sin
- Conversion is when a person turns from their sins and trusts in Jesus alone

Post Conversion Evidence

- Once saved, a Christian receives the free gift of eternal life and will live in eternity with Jesus
- The justified believer desires to please Jesus by following Him and serving Him
- Following Jesus means learning from Jesus and imitating Him as He reveals Himself in the Bible; repenting when you sin, and putting your will and life into Jesus' hands

The Traditional Romans Road to Salvation

Main Message
John 3:16 ESV
> *"For God so loved the world, that he gave his only Son, that whoever believes in him should not perish but have eternal life."*

The Problem of Sin
Romans 3:23 ESV
> *"for all have sinned and fall short of the glory of God,"*

Romans 3:10-18 ESV
> *"as it is written: "None is righteous, no, not one; no one understands; no one seeks for God. All have turned aside; together they have become worthless; no one does good, not even one. Their throat is an open grave; they use their tongues to deceive. The venom of asps is under their lips. Their mouth is full of curses and bitterness. Their feet are swift to shed blood; in their paths are ruin and misery, and the way of peace they have not known. There is no fear of God before their eyes."*

The Punishment
Romans 6:23 ESV
> *"For the wages of sin is death, but the free gift of God is eternal life in Christ Jesus our Lord."*

The Payment
Romans 5:8 ESV
> *"but God shows his love for us in that while we were still sinners, Christ died for us."*

The Response
Romans 10:9-10 ESV

> *"because, if you confess with your mouth that Jesus is Lord and believe in your heart that God raised him from the dead, you will be saved. For with the heart one believes and is justified, and with the mouth one confesses and is saved."*

Romans 10:13 ESV

> *"For "everyone who calls on the name of the Lord will be saved."*

The Reconciliation
Romans 5:1 ESV

> *"Therefore, since we have been justified by faith, we have peace with God through our Lord Jesus Christ."*

The Guarantee
Romans 8:1-2 ESV

> *"There is therefore now no condemnation for those who are in Christ Jesus. For the law of the Spirit of life has set you free in Christ Jesus from the law of sin and death."*

The Promise
Romans 8:35-39 ESV

> *"Who shall separate us from the love of Christ? Shall tribulation, or distress, or persecution, or famine, or nakedness, or danger, or sword? As it is written, "For your sake we are being killed all the day long; we are regarded as sheep to be slaughtered."No, in all these things we are more than conquerors through him who loved us. For I am sure that neither death nor life, nor angels nor rulers, nor things present nor things to come, nor powers, nor height nor depth, nor anything else in all creation, will be able to separate us from the love of God in Christ Jesus our Lord."*

The Missing Part to the Romans Road to Salvation

Part of the problem with the Romans Road to Salvation method is that it leaves out the cost and how we are to live after salvation. While I feel the Romans Road can be helpful, it is very important to include the following verses on repenting and living a changed life.

The Personal Sacrifice

Romans 6:1-2 ESV

> *"What shall we say then? Are we to continue in sin that grace may abound? By no means! How can we who died to sin still live in it?"*

Romans 12:1-2 ESV

> *"I appeal to you therefore, brothers, by the mercies of God, to present your bodies as a living sacrifice, holy and acceptable to God, which is your spiritual worship. Do not be conformed to this world, but be transformed by the renewal of your mind, that by testing you may discern what is the will of God, what is good and acceptable and perfect."*

Three other verses that are important to the gospel outside of the book of Romans are:

The Repentance of Sins

1 John 1:9 ESV

> *"If we confess our sins, he is faithful and just to forgive us our sins and to cleanse us from all unrighteousness."*

Acts 3:19 ESV

> *"Repent therefore, and turn back, that your sins may be blotted out."*

The New Life in Christ

2 Corinthians 5:17 ESV

> *"Therefore, if anyone is in Christ, he is a new creation. The old has passed away; behold, the new has come."*

The Expanded Gospel Message

The following is the gospel message written out to help you solidify your understanding of the good news.

God created everything. He created this earth and everything in it, including you and me. He created us in His image: intelligent, willful, emotional, and moral.

God created us to be holy because He is holy. Holy means to be set apart, to be pure. Adam and Eve were 100% holy and pure at creation. Even though He created Adam and Eve, they decided they knew better. They were deceived into thinking they could control their own lives without God. They insisted that they were right and that God's commands for them were somehow optional, so they did their own thing. They followed their hearts and disobeyed God thinking it wouldn't be that big of a deal. They ate the forbidden fruit, thus cursing all of their offspring. This is why we have a sinful nature. Sin entered the world through our first parents.

That one decision to live outside of God's will (His design) caused us to no longer be pure. We are now on our own; no longer able to be with God. We willfully separated ourselves from God by selfishly desiring to be in control of our own lives.

Our departure from God brought massive consequences. No longer are we following the righteous will of God, but the sinful will of our own flesh. Sin, while often thought of as an act, is also the essence of our nature. Sin means we are no longer holy, we are separated from God, on our own, living for ourselves 100% of the time.

This sin state of being has horrendous ramifications. It manifests itself in different ways for different people. For some, sin shows in big ways that we all know and hate such as murder, rape, and grand theft. However, for the majority of us, it manifests in seemingly smaller ways, such as a white lie to get out of a parking ticket, stealing office supplies from our work, "borrowing" music and movies illegally on the Internet, cheating just a bit (or a lot) on our taxes, making false insurance claims to get a better outcome, gossiping about a friend to make ourselves look better, lusting after a friend's spouse, getting wrapped up in pornography, or making an idol of money. Sin improperly directs how we think about our neighbor, our families, even our very selves.

We fib and stretch the truth and justify our white-collar crimes against God, all in an effort to live a life that seems to be free, but is full of bondage. Sin is a lifestyle marked by self-serving behavior. Again, sin is not only an act, but it is the nature of who we are as humans. It is within the very fiber of our being. Our sin nature, causes our sinful behavior.

God is the ultimate Judge and He is the most just of all judges. He created you, He created me. Because He created us all, that means He has ultimate ownership and authority over us. He can do what He likes with us regardless of what we think or feel because that is what is fair. God views all sin as bad. It must be punished. Sinful acts are an outpouring of our sin nature.

Our desire to be in charge and our desire to do what we want rather than what God, our Creator has asked us to do, deserves punishment. We do not deserve a get-out-of-jail-free card simply because we are "pretty good." He is holy, yet we are no longer holy. We cannot be in the presence of God without judgment or reconciliation.

There needs to be reconciliation in order for us to be right before God again. A created thing that goes rogue deserves to be put to death. We deserve death, which should be our sentence. That is what hell is all about. Hell is our prison cell. We get a glimpse of what it is in the Bible, and believe me, you do not want to go there. Just a few descriptive words about it are enough to make your skin crawl: eternal damnation, weeping, gnashing of teeth, eternal fire, unquenchable thirst. This jail cell is where we are all headed for eternity because of our separation from God.

Here is where the reality of our state gets wildly interesting and almost too incredible for words. God is love. He is not just loving, He does not just love us, but He *is* love. He is the very source of love. Like when you plug in a lamp, you see effects of the energy through the light bulb. The light bulb would be how we understand love. The actual energy that it is plugged into, the source of the energy is what God is like. When you plug into God, it is then that you see the beautiful effects of what we know as love.

His love extended to us in an unimaginable way when He did the unthinkable. He knows we are weak. He knows we need Him. He knows the desires of our flesh are strong. He stepped in and did the one thing we could never do. He came down to live among us perfectly. He sent His only Son, Jesus, God in the flesh, to live a perfect life. Something none of us could ever do. He lived a perfect, sinless life. He was our proxy.

Then, in an inconceivable act of mercy and grace, He died the very death each and every one of us deserve to die as punishment for our sin. He was guiltless. He lived the life we never could only to die the death each of us deserved: a death on a cross. This was a horrendously humiliating, excruciatingly painful and drawn-out death.

He reconciled my life, and if you are a child of God, He reconciled your life back to Him through His death. He paid our penalty. He satisfied the Judge. He stepped in for us! As if that were not enough, Jesus came back to life. He defeated death. He defied nature. He is living proof of what we get to experience some day! That is what grace is all about! Mercy is not getting what we deserve, while grace is getting what we don't deserve.

It almost seems too good to be true! It seems like a great fairytale. But it is real. The veracity of the Bible, the actual life, death, and resurrection of the God-man Jesus has been documented and proven even by those outside of the Christian faith! So why are there millions upon millions of people who still don't believe and may never give their lives to Christ? Our sin nature is so deeply rooted and woven into the fiber of our souls that we want it *not* to be true.

God still gives us a choice. He still gives us our will. Our will wants to satisfy ourself. Our soul cannot and will not bow to another. Before you are saved, the throne room of your heart already has someone firmly planted on its seat: you. Everyone is dead in their sins. A dead person cannot choose to be alive. It is humanly hopeless, but here is hope!

God calls His children. One by one, His Holy Spirit convinces and convicts each of His kids of their sin, of their need for holiness and righteousness, and He presses on their heart the very heavy burden of their sin and need for reconciliation. The Holy Spirit works in the believer, quickening his or her heart to desire after God's heart. He shows His child the reality of his or her sin and the glory and splendor of what it means to be free of that burden. The simple yet profound act of placing one's life in the hands of the Almighty God becomes a 180 degree shift from self to God.

The believer then turns from their idol of self and turns to a life where Jesus is the only One able to sit on the throne of their heart. The white flag is raised, confession is made, and forgiveness is found. There is then a realization that ownership of oneself is not ours, but that of our Creator. It is with a contrite heart that the believer trusts fully in Jesus and follows wholeheartedly after Him knowing others will despise them. As a follower of Jesus, the believer now recognizes the futility of living for oneself and realizes the beauty of a grace and mercy-filled life of living for God.

Friend, if you are on the wrong side of this, I implore you, by the mercy of God, to get reconciled to God. Place your trust and faith in Him alone. Turn away from your sin and yourself and turn to God. The peace, love, mercy, and grace will wrap around your heart and give you courage and strength to follow diligently after Him.

There is no magic prayer. There is no "Ticket to Heaven" only to go back to a self-serving life. If you have raised the white flag of repentance and faith, read the Bible. That is how God speaks to us. Pray all of the time, talk to God, ask for Him to forgive you of your sin. Ask Him to give you faith and wisdom to do His will. Share with others what you have found!

CHAPTER 10

LORDSHIP SALVATION

"For this is the love of God,
that we keep his commandments.
And his commandments are not burdensome."
1 John 5:3 ESV

I was a latch-key kid after my parents got a divorce. My mom would leave me a list of things I had to do before she got home. My job was to finish the list, not question the list. It wasn't a good idea for me to decide for myself what I interpreted the list to say.

A friend of mine says that when she pulls into the parking lot of her work, if she sees her boss's car parked, she immediately sits up straighter in her car even though he is not actually around. It is her instinct to do so. We should feel the same way with God. He is *always* watching but we never consider the simple fact that He is there.

How oddly un-odd it is that I don't think to consider God's omniscience more. He is *everywhere* and yet I have been known to try to excuse my behavior as something out of my control. I may claim that I am overwhelmed and tired, I excuse my self-serving and self-preserving actions at the expense of God's design. That is enough to make me crumble in sadness over my own sin. When does this behavior become a habit? How can we, as Christians, justify making a habit of sin? If I were to casually regard the mercy of God and choose to continue in my sin, am I not condemning myself through this habit? Sanctification is an important area to work through as it pertains to sin. Salvation through the lordship of Jesus helps me to understand the sanctification process, which we will discuss in the next chapter. For now, I would like to define what lordship salvation is and how it contrasts with easy-believism.

There are basically two types of Christians I would like to discuss in this chapter: those who feel they are saved simply because they believe, and that they can go on sinning and living for themselves, or those who understand that their life is no longer their own and that they must follow the commands that God has given them. The former is called easy-believism and the latter Lordship salvation. Let me be really clear here. The former is not saved.

Easy-believism sometimes falls into the trap of name-it-and-claim-it theology or prosperity gospel. It is a simplified version of "ignorance is bliss" or "glass half full." While there is something to be desired from this type of thinking, when it is applied to the gospel, it discounts the harder truths and reaches into easy-believism. Prosperity gospel is where a person truly feels that they should always be blessed by God and that they are a daughter or son of the King; therefore, a princess or prince that deserves the best. This is like the bratty rich kid who wants his or her inheritance before their parents die, like the prodigal son story in the Bible. (Luke 15:11-32) Nowhere in the Bible does it say becoming a

Christian will be easy and that all of your problems will go away. In fact, the opposite is true! Let's investigate:

"For it has been granted to you that for the sake of Christ you should not only believe in him but also suffer for his sake," (Philippians 1:29 ESV)

"Count it all joy, my brothers, when you meet trials of various kinds, for you know that the testing of your faith produces steadfastness. And let steadfastness have its full effect, that you may be perfect and complete, lacking in nothing." (James 1:2-4 ESV)

"More than that, we rejoice in our sufferings, knowing that suffering produces endurance, and endurance produces character, and character produces hope, and hope does not put us to shame, because God's love has been poured into our hearts through the Holy Spirit who has been given to us." (Romans 5:3-5 ESV)

"For I consider that the sufferings of this present time are not worth comparing with the glory that is to be revealed to us." (Romans 8:18 ESV)

"Beloved, do not be surprised at the fiery trial when it comes upon you to test you, as though something strange were happening to you. But rejoice insofar as you share Christ's sufferings, that you may also rejoice and be glad when his glory is revealed." (1 Peter 4:12-13 ESV)

"Indeed, all who desire to live a godly life in Christ Jesus will be persecuted," (2 Timothy 3:12 ESV)

If those verses were not enough to make you count the cost of being a Christian, I do not know what will. Life was never promised to be easy for us as Christians or anyone for that matter. In fact, life will be hard. Sometimes, really hard.

Here in the United States, especially in Southern California, and even more so in South Orange County, life seems so easy. Living here I often joke that our problems are "first world problems" such as the argument over what restaurant to go to, or who needs to pick up the dry cleaning. There are real complaints too, such as, "I have too much going on, my schedule is so overwhelmed that I can never find any time to do anything for myself." "I'm so tired all the time and have no patience for my kids. All I do is yell at them constantly."

These comments are from stay-at-home moms who, one would think, have more comfortable lives than most. Yet, people are worn out wherever they live and whatever circumstances they live under. The big difference I find is in hope. Christians have a sure and firm hope. Even though things may be bad and we go through trials, we still have assurance. People who have a wishful hope are the ones I fear for the most. By "wishful hope" I mean someone who has a "cross your fingers and hope it's true" kind of hope.

When I look back at my pre-salvific life (before I was saved,) I see a life full of abundance and things going my way. When I was living those moments, I thought things were hard. I had to work really hard to get ahead, but ahead I always got. My life was filled with things of this world that were dazzling, both in relationships and objects.

Now, post-salvation, my life is way harder than I would have ever thought possible. Things no longer "come easy" and trials and tests seem to be around every corner. God is sharpening, pruning, and disciplining me week after week. It is a brutal but necessary part of being a child of God.

Sharpening hurts. There is heat and sparks that fly but in the end I am becoming more and more sharp in my walk with God. I am sharpened with the searing pain of feeling the effect of my words on others and how to speak with more mercy and grace. I am sharpened when I feel the pride-crushing agony of learning to submit to my authorities and leaders. I am again sharpened as I understand the level of commitment it takes to be an ambassador of Christ. This is what it means to be a follower of Jesus - Lordship salvation.

Pruning is painful, yet the outcome is beautiful. There are things I did not even consider a barrier to loving God that are now a full-blown assault on my walk. The daily barrage on my spirit with the conflict of time-wasting activities. I am pruned when I feel the struggle of giving up certain foods that God revealed to me are emotionally damaging. I am pruned with true sadness in losing friends and a career over following Jesus. When I am pruned, I can feel my life conforming more and more to the Lord. Pruning allows for more beautiful and abundant growth.

Jesus asked us to simply follow His commands. He asked us to love one another as He has loved us. He asked you, He asked me! He asked us to do everything as if we were doing it to Him and for Him personally. Yikes, that is not the case in my everyday life, is it in yours? I hope that we could all resolve to consider God's presence in our lives as much as possible. I desire to consider my conversations, thoughts, and even my mindless facial expression to others that may be hurtful. My goal is to consistently take another step closer in my own quest to undomesticate God and continue my journey toward loving others and completing tasks with the weight of God's omniscience! Are you with me?

True Christianity is not a popular belief, but domesticated Christianity is very much so. It confuses me when I hear other "church-goers" say, "Oh, you are a really dedicated Christian," or "You are one of those all-in Christians." Is there anything other than an "all-in" Christian according to Jesus?

Thinking there are different levels of being a Christian is a gross domestication of God. In reality it is very black and white. A true Christian is consistent. Not consistently perfect, but consistently humble to the working of the Holy Spirit through the Word of God. They live a life of repentance, always seeking the Lord. There are people I know who label themselves as all-in Jesus followers, yet are consistently gossiping, slandering others, using foul language, supporting anti-Christian activities, lying, cheating, and even using Jesus as a way to sell their products. It breaks my heart and while I do not know if they are truly saved or not, it makes me wonder if the Holy Spirit is in them and they are quenching Him or if Satan has deceived them in such a way as to cause them to be blind.

We will sin, that is for certain, but if we make a habit of sin, that is where I would ask you to consider if the Holy Spirit is actually inside of you.

> *"This is the message we have heard from him and proclaim to you, that God is light, and in him is no darkness at all."*
> (1 John 1:5 ESV)

God is light without any darkness. Typically, there are two meanings for light and dark: the intellectual and the moral. Intellectually, light is truth and darkness is falsehood. Morally, light is purity and darkness is sin. In the above verse in 1

John 1:5, John is challenging the heretics of the day who met in secret societies cloaked in rituals and veiled initiation rites. For them to claim they knew God was ridiculous because God is light and He would not be found in the literal dark rituals of the heretics.

The concept of evil is interesting for today's modern society where so much is applauded that is shrouded in darkness and secrecy. My heart breaks when I see kids, and even my own son, playing a video game where he is cheered on when he gets more "head shots" than anyone else in the game. Killing others, and dancing on them in victory is desensitizing my own child and making light of something that is very dark.

For years I got sucked into watching TV series on the occult. From vampires to witches and werewolves, it was all so fascinating to me. I still catch myself being interested in the themes of vampires, as the idea of living forever is written on our hearts. (Ecclesiastes 3:11) Through the media, this beautiful truth of eternal life with Jesus has been twisted into a darkness no one would ever want: living forever destined to feed off of the blood of humans.

It is easier for those who participate in evil to live in the darkness too. What is truth these days? From political lies and scandals to gray areas of sin such as drinking, dating, gambling, smoking, clothing, music, etc. How do we, as Christians, discern the difference between right and wrong, good and evil?

I grew up in a church where the leadership team looked the other way when confronted with bold-faced sin. There was no accountability and sin was shrouded in secrecy. This was a supposedly Bible-teaching Baptist church. After I left for college, one person after another fell into scandal. BIG scandal. It was like watching flies drop, starting with the man behind the pulpit to the one leading worship to the youth minister and on and on. It was horrific, sad, and heartbreaking. How does that much scandal happen in one church? Secrecy. Sin. Darkness.

We all sin, but it is the fact of making sin a practice that is the difference. Making a habit of sin is what John expands upon in 1 John 3:6.

"No one who abides in him keeps on sinning; no one who keeps on sinning has either seen him or known him."
(1 John 3:6 ESV)

"If we say we have no sin, we deceive ourselves, and the truth is not in us." (1 John 1:8 ESV)

If you practice sin continually, John, without hesitation, calls us out as not being a Christian. We will stumble. But with the Holy Spirit in us, it is extremely hard, impossible really, to make a practice of sin. Take a moment to read the five short chapters of 1 John. Reading these five chapters will most likely either convict you or confirm you of your own salvation. 1 John is a good place to start when working through understanding what Lordship salvation is.

CHAPTER 11

SANCTIFICATION

*"Therefore, my beloved, as you have always obeyed, so now,
not only as in my presence but much more in my absence,
work out your own salvation with fear and trembling,"*
Philippians 2:12 ESV

Fear and trembling! Those are not easy words; they are intense. The letter to the Philippians was intended for those Paul considered to already be saved. He was encouraging his brothers and sisters in Christ to work out their sanctification.

The Greek word for our English translated "salvation" is sōtēria, which is the present possession of God's mercy and grace for those who are His children. Because this letter was written to those who were Christians, Paul was encouraging them to pay close attention to their sanctification.

There are two words that are important to the Christian faith: justification and sanctification. When you are saved, at the moment of conversion, you are justified. This means you are made right before God. Your sins have been forgiven. As you move through your life as a justified Christian, you will quickly realize just how heavy your sin is, and how present it still is.

When you are saved, you do not automatically become a perfect person. This is what sanctification is about. It is the act of becoming more and more like Christ. This side of heaven, no person will ever be perfect. We are justified at salvation, but are a work in progress through sanctification as God reveals, step by step, the sins in our lives that we need to work on. This is one part of the sanctification process.

God has blessed me by teaching, correcting, and training me in righteousness through my own sanctification. If I encountered all of my sin all at once, I would not be able to move forward. My shame and guilt would overcome me so utterly that all I could do is lay prostrate on the ground in submission to a holy God.

I recently moved a plant to a new location near a sunny window in my home. Of course I wanted to see the beautiful leaves so I turned it toward me. After a day I noticed the leaves had all turned toward the light. So, I turned it back. I sat there for about 10 minutes watching it. Nothing. I left and came back after several hours. Sure enough the leaves were all turned again. Sometimes in our walk with God we cannot see the immediate effects of our sanctification. We want instant gratification, or as some call it, "rapid sanctification" or "aggressive sanctification." We want to see change before our eyes. Yes, occasionally we get to see change that smacks us in the face, but more often than not, our sanctification, our growth and turning toward God's light, is gradual to us. Ask a friend or a family member if you are changing and growing in Christ (our light). They may have a better perspective.

If you want to do a deeper dive to figure out if you are indeed being sanctified, there are some simple audits you can do on yourself. Consider your feelings, actions, and motives when it comes to Jesus. Let me ask you a seemingly simple question. How do you feel about Jesus? Does the following describe you?

- You believe in Jesus
- You love Jesus
- You have put your faith and trust in Him
- You have tried to turn from your sinful ways and toward righteousness
- You go to church
- You volunteer
- You pray
- You read your Bible

That is great! Welcome to eternal salvation. Well... hold on. Our response to the free gift of salvation is an orientation of the heart. It is revealed in our motives and will overflow in our actions. Put yourself against these scenarios, many of which most of us fail in, myself included. How can we consider the motives of our heart and what flows from it?

- You are at work, you are on your break at your desk reading your Bible. How do you react when you hear someone coming? Do you quickly close your Bible or do you keep reading?
- You are at a restaurant with Christian friends. Do you pray before a meal or do you pass it up for lighter conversation?
- Do you ever pray for an extended period of time with another friend out in public?

- You are at work in the lunchroom. Do you pray before your meal in front of everyone or do you quietly pray in your mind without anyone being the wiser?

- You are at a social event and someone you have never met asks you what you do. Do you bring up your reason for living by bringing up Jesus or do you talk endlessly about what you do for a monetary living?

- You are at the park with a friend who is definitely not a Christian (make it more real and imagine your Muslim, Buddhist, or outspoken atheist friend), and you casually tuck your cross necklace into your shirt before you see them for fear of confrontation.

- You are at your kids school picking them up and you get into a conversation with another mom. Does the name of Jesus ever come into your conversations?

- Generally speaking, how often does the name Jesus enter into your daily conversation with those around you? For me personally, I must be intentional and considerate of the Holy Spirit's promptings.

We sing songs about "Jesus, only Jesus" but then are afraid to mention His name in mixed company for fear we will lose our jobs, lose a friend, or lose respect. We think in our hearts, "I cannot wait to see the face of Jesus shining like the sun," but then can't seem to say His name to others during the course of our day.

Is this how you treat someone you love? When you are in love you want to shout it from the mountaintops. When you find your spouse you cannot wait to introduce them to everyone and anyone. When you have your first, second, third, twelfth grandchild, how quick are you to whip out those photos of them even to perfect strangers? But Jesus? No, that is not politically correct.

Ask yourself: "How do I *really* feel about Jesus?" The world sends thousands of signals to us like little darts all intended for us to dislike or even hate Jesus. We are in a literal battlefield. If only we could see what the angels see. Take a look at what the Bible says about it.

> *"For everyone who has been born of God overcomes the world. And this is the victory that has overcome the world—our faith. Who is it that overcomes the world except the one who believes that Jesus is the Son of God?"* (1 John 5:4-5 ESV)

> *"So everyone who acknowledges me before men, I also will acknowledge before my Father who is in heaven, but whoever denies me before men, I also will deny before my Father who is in heaven."* (Matthew 10:32-33 ESV)

You may be tempted to think that people really don't want to hear about Jesus. I hear excuses like,

- "I don't want to offend anyone."
- "I'm terrible at going up to people."
- "I believe what I believe and I let others believe what they want to believe."
- "I never know what to say, I am afraid I will stumble with my words and make Christianity look dumb."
- "Evangelizing is okay for pastors, but I don't feel called to do it and besides I'm no good at it anyway."

These are just a few of the excuses I have used, and have heard other people use as well. Do you realize that if Paul, Peter, James or any of the other apostles and disciples felt this way and acted on their feelings, no one would have heard the gospel? Sure, the rocks would cry out if they were silent, but God desires our involvement in His plan.

> *"He answered, "I tell you, if these were silent, the very stones would cry out."* (Luke 19:40 ESV)

We must remember that *we* are the ones that need to preach the good news!

> *"How then will they call on him in whom they have not believed? And how are they to believe in him of whom they have never heard? And how are they to hear without someone preaching?"* (Romans 10:14 ESV)

Jesus did not ask only His first disciples to share the gospel, He asked everyone who calls himself or herself a believer and follower of Christ to share the gospel. The Holy Spirit helps us but we must be willing to be His ambassador. We are privileged to help God in the calling of His people.

"But I honestly don't know how to share the gospel." This is a valid response, however if your child said, "but I don't know how to read," would you just stop and say, "You know what? I get it. It is just too hard and confusing for you. Don't worry about it then. You will be fine…"? We know that would never happen, so we need to act like adults and do what our Father has asked us to do. Here is a short list that will help you get started.

1. Practice
You will never get good at anything unless you practice. Person by person. Start today with just one person.

2. Be Prepared
You need to know what you are sharing. Going around saying to people they need God because He will make their lives better and that He loves them is not the best place to start. If you understand the costs associated with following Christ, then you are more able to explain the full gospel to someone else. A great place to learn how to share the gospel is at: www.sharetheumbrella.com.

3. Understand Your Role
It may not be effective to go up to people and say, "Do you want to hear about Jesus?" Think about the last time you bought something that was sold to you. Why did you buy it? You did not just wake up and decide, "I'm going to buy a new car today." There would have been some great marketing done by the company along with your own forethought and research to back up your purchase.

We do business with people we know, like, and trust. Don't assume spreading the gospel is any different than selling anything else. I don't want to cheapen the gospel by any means, but I do want you to think about it the next time you try to shove your religion down someone's throat. It never works. There will be times when someone will flat out ask you to share, point-by-point, what the gospel is. However, more often than not, people will be drawn to your "light" because of your love and the way you live your life, which, in turn, will afford you the ability to openly share the gospel message.

Look for opportunities to share a little bit of Jesus in every conversation. Literally try to think, "How can I mention the name of Jesus in this conversation?" You will start getting good at inserting the Word of God in all of your conversations.

4. Pray, Pray, and Pray Some More

- Ask God every morning for "divine appointments" to share God's Word.

- Ask God for "low hanging fruit," which are people who want to talk about Jesus who may not know Him yet.

- Ask the Holy Spirit to speak through you.

- Any time you share the gospel or are building a relationship with someone, pray for them often, even in your mind during conversations with that person.

- When you share the gospel with others, pray regularly for them. Pray that the Holy Spirit would do a great work in them and bring them to repentance and faith.

Don't ever forget, Jesus calls us as His ambassadors to "make disciples." Making disciples may be sharing the gospel and helping to bring about conversion or it may mean helping to teach a new believer how to grow in his or her faith. Either way, making and growing disciples is our call as believers.

> *"Go therefore and make disciples of all nations, baptizing them in the name of the Father and of the Son and of the Holy Spirit,"* (Matthew 28:19 ESV)

> *"Therefore, we are ambassadors for Christ, God making his appeal through us. We implore you on behalf of Christ, be reconciled to God."* (2 Corinthians 5:20 ESV)

As you get more comfortable sharing Jesus in your everyday conversations, you will also want to consider how others see you in your walk.

The more time you spend with God, the closer you will become to Him and the more you will want to spend time with Him. Imagine getting to a place where you no longer need to "carve out" time in your life for God, but where you need to carve out time in your walk with God for your life. The Lord promises that if you hunger and thirst to do His will, obey His commands, and follow after Him, you will be satisfied.

"Blessed are those who hunger and thirst for righteousness, for they shall be satisfied." (Matthew 5:6 ESV)

In fact, you will be more than satisfied. Take a look at what Peter has to say:

"Though you have not seen him, you love him. Though you do not now see him, you believe in him and rejoice with joy that is inexpressible and filled with glory," (1 Peter 1:8 ESV)

In Peter's day, his readers understood the word "agapo" or "love" to mean continually loving God as a regular daily activity. The word "pisteuo" or "believe" means to rest your confidence in or to trust in or depend on. The joy of this verse implies joy for the present. The word for rejoice was not commonly used by secular Greek writers during this time period, as it meant a deep spiritual joy. As we continually spend time daily with Jesus, through faith, we rejoice all the more. The original readers understood this as wanting more and more of Jesus and that joy was something only believers could experience. Have you experienced this?

Even though I have not seen Jesus, I am active in my love for Him and faith in Him by daily worshiping Him through prayer and Bible reading. Because of this communion with Jesus, I have even deeper joy that is filled with the glory of heaven. By adjusting your life to focus more on God, you will inevitably begin to mirror the following passage written by Paul to the Galatians.

> *"But I say, walk by the Spirit, and you will not gratify the desires of the flesh. For the desires of the flesh are against the Spirit, and the desires of the Spirit are against the flesh, for these are opposed to each other, to keep you from doing the things you want to do. But if you are led by the Spirit, you are not under the law. Now the works of the flesh are evident: sexual immorality, impurity, sensuality, idolatry, sorcery, enmity, strife, jealousy, fits of anger, rivalries, dissensions, divisions, envy, drunkenness, orgies, and things like these. I warn you, as I warned you before, that those who do such things will not inherit the kingdom of God. But the fruit of the Spirit is love, joy, peace, patience, kindness, goodness, faithfulness, gentleness, self-control; against such things there is no law. And those who belong to Christ Jesus have crucified the flesh with its passions and desires. If we live by the Spirit, let us also walk by the Spirit. Let us not become conceited, provoking one another, envying one another."* (Galatians 5:16-26 ESV)

The reality is, we are really good at deceiving others, and most importantly ourselves. I honestly wish we could all experience the joy, blessing, and honor it is to truly know Jesus. The fact of the matter is, many people who identify with Christianity are simply lying to others and themselves without even knowing it.

> *"If we say we have fellowship with him while we walk in darkness, we lie and do not practice the truth."* (1 John 1:6 ESV)

Fellowship (the Greek word koinōnia) is used in 1 John 1:6 in relation to God. It meant to have intimacy with God. This was a foreign concept to the Jews and those of other religions because the word koinōnia to them simply meant to have community or joint participation with others. In context of 1 John, Christians understood that "fellowship with God" meant that they now have access to the Father through the Son. The literal and figurative veil was torn at the death and sacrifice of Jesus Christ. The resurrection and the following receiving of the Holy Spirit guaranteed and sealed their fellowship.

A deceived Christian might say he or she is intimate with Jesus. They might say they love Him and think He loves them back. The giveaway that this warped sense of reality is, in fact, not true, is when someone claims Christ as the one they follow, yet walks in darkness.

The phrase "walk in" as seen in 1 John 1:6 in Greek is περιπατέω. This word is transliterated as "peripateō," which means "to walk," however John used this word to mean the conduct of one's life. I realize that we often speak of ourselves or others as having lost their way, but John is clear. He says if someone says they are a Christian, but the habitual conduct of their life is counter to God's word, then they are not a Christian. At all.

"If we say we have no sin, we deceive ourselves, and the truth is not in us." (1 John 1:8 ESV)

Remember, Satan has had thousands of years to perfect the art of deception, and you better believe he is excellent at his craft. Don't believe the lie he is telling you. Start looking at your life through Truth; through what the Bible has to say.

Please do not lie to yourself thinking you are better than the next person. While you may be a good person, what does that actually mean? I want to give you some solid examples rather than leave this up to interpretation. Here is a very short list of typical justifications of sins people who call themselves Christians commit in our entitled world.

Justification #1
Person one is sleeping with her boyfriend. (I am going to expand on this first one just a bit so you can see what I mean). She has somehow decided that God asking her to wait until she is married is either antiquated or she feels that because she is engaged that God won't mind.
(1 Corinthians 7:2, Hebrews 13:4, 1 Thessalonians 4:3-5)

I remember having a long conversation with an older man in my neighborhood who identified so strongly with Jesus and was extremely involved in his church. He was divorced with kids and was dating another woman from his church who was also divorced with kids. In the conversation he mentioned three things:

1. They are living together.
2. Yes, they are sleeping together, but they said vows to each other so in the eyes of God they are married.
3. They are not getting along so he thinks he is going to break up with her soon.

WHAT?? I could have just left it alone, but I called him out on his obvious erroneous thought process. He believed so many lies and was living one HUGE lie after another. He sort of ho-hum agreed with my rebuke, and I never saw him again.

Another person in my life shared that she feels justified that she and her boyfriend are sleeping together because they are getting married soon and have also stated some sort of private vows. Not only is that unbiblical on several levels, it is also an issue because they were sleeping together LONG before they ever even started to talk about getting married. She agrees to disagree with me and is no longer speaking to me.

A woman believes the man she is marrying will "come around." She says he promised to come to church with her and she is hopeful he will get saved soon. She also says that she can walk down the aisle, say her vows, and then ask God to forgive her for going against His word by becoming unequally yoked. This last example was the lie I told myself before I got married.

How are all of these lies becoming truths? Satan is hard at work deceiving everyone he possibly can.

Justification #2
Person two calls herself a "cussin' Christian."
She uses bad words. Often. Perhaps she uses the Lord's Name in vain and really doesn't think much of it. She has chosen to disregard the Bible's teachings on this. This is all a lie she is telling herself.
(Colossians 3:8, Ephesians 4:29, Exodus 10:7)

Justification #3
Person three considers herself a prayer warrior. She says her gift is not evangelism and has decided to leave that to people who are gifted at talking to strangers or who are gifted at sharing the gospel with others. Besides, that gift is for pastors and people in full-time ministry. Again, another lie. We *all* are commissioned to spread the gospel. ALL.
(2 Corinthians 5:20, Matthew 28:19-20, Romans 10:15)

Justification #4

Person four considers herself a normal Christian, but has friends who she calls "Jesus Freaks." She reserves that name for the really intense Christians in her life, but that is not her at all. She fits in. Her way of witnessing to others is by not being crazy, because who is really going to respond to that anyway, right? LIE!! Being a Jesus Freak does not mean being out of your mind crazy. It means living a life that is counter to how the world lives; living based on the Bible. Yes, that would most likely put you in the Jesus Freak category, but not in the, stand-on-the-street-corner-holding-an-end-of-the-world-sign type of crazy. (Luke 9:23, Galatians 2:20, Matthew 25:21)

Justification #5

Person five attends church, reads the Bible, goes on short term missions, and gives offering to the church. She made a profession of faith when she was 13, she got baptized and she is from a Christian family. Christianity is not a checklist. While these things should flow from the heart of the truly saved, these things, in and of themselves, do not make you a Christian. Check your growth. Check your fruit.
(Matthew 23:27-28, 2 Corinthians 13:5, Philippians 2:12)

Justification #6

Person six always seems to not have enough money and is trying to get more. She tells herself it is not money that is bad, it is the *love* of money. While yes, that is true, desiring after money is still a lie. If you are chasing money and using that line to back up your idol, then again you are living a lie.
(Hebrews 13:5, 1 Timothy 6:9-10, Ecclesiastes 5:10)

Because "Justification #6" is a common one for many of us, I would like to spend more time discussing money. Have you ever considered that we live in a world where we sit in a Starbucks sipping a $4 latte and complain about how we lost a stock investment or that our kid's tuition for private school is too high, or that the price of gas is over $4 a gallon in Los Angeles, California? Did you know that over half the population of the world lives on less than $2 a day? We are rich beyond what we could even understand rich to mean.

I sat in a Bible study several years ago and listened to an Orange County housewife pour her heart out to the group that she was desperate for prayer because her family was, in her words, "one paycheck away from being homeless." I honestly did not know what to say. Did she even understand what the word "homeless" meant? God forbid she cut back on her cable bill or cancel her cellphone service. But hey, let's decide we are going to be homeless because we won't be able to afford the $8,000 a month in household expenses! My initial instinct was outrage, but then realized this is how most people live. It is how *I* lived! People in my area don't understand how anyone else lives on $100 a day let alone $2. How could they? All they know is this life they live. People want what they are used to. It made me realize just how beholden I was to my own finances.

It was then that I started to take a look around. I looked at my checking account to see what I spent my money on. I wanted to find out what was most important to me and my family. I realized that I was obsessed. Obsessed with the things of this world. I had to have the most high-end accessories and the most expensive shoes. My car needed to be a luxury model. My hair had to be perfect all of the time with the perfect highlights. I was spending tons of cash on things that had zero eternal value.

There was never a day that I stepped out of my house without makeup. I was indeed obsessed. My obsession was not really in the things themselves, as those are not the sin. My sin was in my motive. I was motivated by how these "things" made me *feel*. I felt better than everyone else when I wore certain affluent marker items. I felt better than others when they did not even know what the brands were that I owned because I was "in the know" and they were not.

I was disgusting! I bought into the lure and the lie of this world. It blinded me to what was really important. Jesus. Jesus, only Jesus. Money is not evil. Desiring after it is. Money is a necessary tool and that is all it is. I am not saying you cannot be a Christian if you have a ton of cash. However, the Bible does have something to say about it.

> *"It is easier for a camel to go through the eye of a needle than for a rich person to enter the kingdom of God."*
> (Mark 10:25 ESV)

Part of the issue with how we read the Bible today is that we do not place it in historical context. If we read Mark 10:25 as literal, it would mean it would be IMPOSSIBLE for a rich person to enter the kingdom of God. Let's take a look at how some people have tried to make this verse fit into a world where it *is* possible for a camel to fit through the eye of a needle. These people claim that a literal eye of a needle is not what Jesus meant at all. They have concocted a legend that there was a really small gate in Jerusalem that was extremely hard for camels to get through. This has never been verified or found to be historically true. I feel this is an attempt by rich people to try to skew Jesus' words in their favor. Here is what Wikipedia says about it.

"The 'eye of the needle' has been claimed to be a gate in Jerusalem, which opened after the main gate was closed at night. A camel could only pass through this smaller gate if it was stooped and had its baggage removed. This story has been put forth since at least the 15th century, and possibly as far back as the 9th century. However, there is no evidence for the existence of such a gate."

Variations on this story include that of ancient inns having small entrances to thwart thieves, or a story of an old mountain pass known as the "eye of the needle," so narrow that merchants would have to dismount from their camels and were thus more vulnerable to waiting brigands. There is no historical evidence for any of these, either. This also ignores the explanation given: "With man this is impossible, but with God all things are possible."

If we take God's Word for what it is, and read Mark 10:25-27, we see that those Jesus was speaking to asked Him, *"Then who can be saved?" Jesus looked at them and said, "With man it is impossible, but not with God. For all things are possible with God."* The point Jesus was making was that it *is* impossible. If you keep reading you will see how it can be made possible for a wealthy person to get to heaven. Here is the full passage so you can see the context.

> *"It is easier for a camel to go through the eye of a needle than for a rich person to enter the kingdom of God." And they were exceedingly astonished, and said to him, "Then who can be saved?" Jesus looked at them and said, "With man it is impossible, but not with God. For all things are possible with God."* (Mark 10:25-27 ESV)

105

Did you catch that? They were exceedingly astonished. I was in another Bible study one evening and brought up this point to another group of wealthy Orange County, California, churchgoers. I thought I was going to get pitch-forked right out of my seat. One woman in front of me actually hit my leg hard in outrage while three others literally whipped around in their seats in horror and disagreement.

Take it up with God people! It is not my opinion. The Word of God is clear. Wealth makes us self-reliant, not God-reliant. Wealth gives us the ability to be distracted. With God, ALL things are possible and I do know some extremely affluent people who are full fledged converts to Christ who follow Him boldly. Interestingly those people are few and they do massive and mighty works for God. They do not tithe to God. They tithe to themselves. They give 10% of what they make to themselves and give 90% back to God through church giving, church planting, and spreading the gospel throughout the world.

Can you take a really good look at your life? Can you find out if you love your life and the things in it just a bit more than God? Can you be honest with yourself?

The following are some great Bible verses to help you consider how money can affect life negatively.

> *"Do not love the world or the things in the world. If anyone loves the world, the love of the Father is not in him. For all that is in the world- the desires of the flesh and the desires of the eyes and pride in possessions-is not from the Father but is from the world. And the world is passing away along with its desires, but whoever does the will of God abides forever."*
> (1 John 2:15-17 ESV)

"If you were of the world, the world would love you as its own; but because you are not of the world, but I chose you out of the world, therefore the world hates you." (John 15:19 ESV)

"No one can serve two masters, for either he will hate the one and love the other, or he will be devoted to the one and despise the other. You cannot serve God and money." (Matthew 6:24 ESV)

"For the love of money is a root of all kinds of evils. It is through this craving that some have wandered away from the faith and pierced themselves with many pangs." (1 Timothy 6:10 ESV)

"Keep your life free from love of money, and be content with what you have, for he has said, "I will never leave you nor forsake you." (Hebrews 13:5 ESV)

"but the cares of the world and the deceitfulness of riches and the desires for other things enter in and choke the word, and it proves unfruitful." (Mark 4:19 ESV)

Everyone tells themselves lies. It is part of our sin nature. We all want to feel like we are justified. Being a Christian means putting aside the things of this world and desiring the things of Jesus. Are you moving one step closer to Jesus today? I must be clear, dear reader, I am not preaching "works salvation." I fear too many people get caught up in trying so desperately to justify their sins, they claim that the person who is convicting them is preaching "works salvation." My friend, Satan is crafty. He will do whatever it takes to keep a single person from true salvation, and he is actually quite happy when even one of God's children becomes slothful in their life for God.

The crushing love of Jesus is what breaks through the barrier that Satan is trying to build. Love is one of the most important elements to understanding your relationship with Jesus.

CHAPTER 12

LOVE

....

"Love is patient and kind; love does not envy or boast; it is not arrogant or rude. It does not insist on its own way; it is not irritable or resentful; it does not rejoice at wrongdoing, but rejoices with the truth. Love bears all things, believes all things, hopes all things, endures all things."
1 Corinthians 13:4-7 ESV

Take a moment to look at the following scripture and replace the word love with your name.

(YOUR NAME HERE)

_____ is patient
_____ is kind
_____ does not envy
_____ does not boast
_____ is not arrogant
_____ is not rude
_____ does not insist on his/her own way
_____ is not irritable
_____ is not resentful
_____ does not rejoice at wrongdoing
_____ rejoices with the truth
_____ bears all things
_____ believes all things
_____ hopes all things
_____ endures all things

*"Teacher, which is the great commandment in the Law?" And
he said to him, "You shall love the Lord your God with all
your heart and with all your soul and with all your mind. This
is the great and first commandment."*
(Matthew 22:36-38 ESV)

Have you ever had an insatiable appetite for something?
Chocolate cake, a hot-off-the-conveyor-belt donut, cold
water after a five-mile run, the book of Revelation, your bed
after dancing all night with your girlfriends, wait, back up,
Revelation? What??? Yes, Revelation. Think about it. Have
you ever been obsessed with reading your Bible? Have you
hungered after it like a newborn is desperate for milk? Here's
what Peter says about it, *"Like newborn infants, long for the pure
spiritual milk, that by it you may grow up into salvation- if indeed
you have tasted that the Lord is good."* (1 Peter 2:2-3 ESV)

The pure spiritual milk Peter is talking about, in the above
verse, is the Word of God. I try to consider what drives my life?
What do I have an appetite for? Where do I spend most of my
time? As the old saying goes, "You are what you eat." When I
go on a diet, the first thing I usually have to do is start tracking
everything I eat. I have to write down each day what I eat, how
much I eat, and how many calories I eat. I cannot know what
to change until I know what my current habits are. I do this
with my finances, too, by tracking where every penny goes.
May I challenge you to do two things.

Taking inventory of where my extra time and money goes
helps me see what is really important to me. I often hear
pastors state that we need to "carve out time for God
everyday." Is carving out 15 minutes or perhaps even 30

minutes a day with my Creator fair when I am spending four hours watching TV, two hours reading novels, and four hours on social media? Pastor Ric Rodeheaver said, "Do not be distracted from the things that matter most by the things that matter least." Here is how I have tried to challenge myself in this area:

- If I watch two hours of TV a day, then I need to consider redeeming that time by spending one hour watching TV and one hour reading my Bible.

- If I spend two hours a day commuting to and from work, then I need to try spending 30 minutes each way praying out loud to God in the car or listening to the Bible on my phone app.

- If I spend one hour reading fiction or thumbing through magazines, I will split that time and spend 30 minutes in a Bible commentary learning something new about God.

- If I workout at the gym for one hour a day, I re-route that endeavor by going on a walk with God in prayer or listening to a sermon while I workout.

These are some of the things I try to do, and I am sure you could come up with some good ideas yourself. The goal is to help you fall more and more in love with God and His Word, but what about His people? People are hard, right? They can be rude and arrogant, they can crush your spirit, they don't do things the way you want them to, they never seem to help you, but you are always bending over backwards for them... the list can go on and on. People are messy, myself among the worst offenders. Let's take a look at a passage:

"Beloved, let us love one another, for love is from God, and whoever loves has been born of God and knows God. Anyone who does not love does not know God, because God is love. In this the love of God was made manifest among us, that God sent his only Son into the world, so that we might live through him. In this is love, not that we have loved God but that he loved us and sent his Son to be the propitiation for our sins. Beloved, if God so loved us, we also ought to love one another. No one has ever seen God; if we love one another, God abides in us and his love is perfected in us." (1 John 4:7-12 ESV)

For a long time I really did not know what to do with the above passage. While I understood the command and the concept, I failed miserably at its application. I wanted to love people, but I somehow always felt destined to not get this right. At my core, I have a hard time relating to people in a loving way. I don't have many friends (a fact my husband keeps telling me to stop sharing.) People throughout my entire life have always let me down. I have trust issues, so I rarely let people in. This is hard for me to admit, as people who know me, know that I am pretty happy and always willing to help others, but what they don't know is that inside I have a running dialogue with myself to beware of other's intentions and always expect others to disappoint me.

One of my students summed it up one night after class when she said, "You are very patient with your students, always eager to explain and re-explain a concept until we get it. But one thing I also know is that you do not suffer fools." That one comment stumped me. As I drove home, I thought long and hard about her comment. She nailed it. I love teaching and really have no problem talking through something several times with patience. However, and it is a big HOWEVER, whenever I get a student in class that is foolish, meaning they really don't care to understand, well, then I have absolutely zero patience for them. I loath people like that. Or at least I did. The word "idiot" often entered my train of thought.

I often found myself in the exact same position as the Pharisee in Jesus' day.

"The Pharisee, standing by himself, prayed thus: 'God, I thank you that I am not like other men, extortioners, unjust, adulterers, or even like this tax collector.'" (Luke 18:11 ESV)

I would just change out the words a bit, such as "Thank you God that I am not like these idiots, or that moron over there who can't seem to get my order right, or that parent that yells at her kids incessantly, or that photographer who has no idea what they are doing." The list is long for me and I bet it is for you, too.

All we know is all we know and usually our way is the best way, right? It is how we were raised and what is ingrained so deeply within us, but God commands us to live a different way. I knew that in my head, but for some reason could not get my heart to line up. When I was honest, I really did feel like a better person than everyone else, but looking back, I was in the darkness.

"Whoever loves his brother abides in the light, and in him there is no cause for stumbling. But whoever hates his brother is in the darkness and walks in the darkness, and does not know where he is going, because the darkness has blinded his eyes." (1 John 2:10-11 ESV)

I was blinded and had no idea why. I was a good "Christian" who prayed, read her Bible, and went to Church. Then I realized, I was trying to do it on my own and not through Christ. Did you know it is almost impossible to love others more than yourself? Even though it is a command, it is something that without the Holy Spirit in our life we cannot do on our own. It is not in our make-up.

> *"Do nothing from selfish ambition or conceit, but in humility count others more significant than yourselves."*
> (Philippians 2:3 ESV)

> *"A new commandment I give to you, that you love one another: just as I have loved you, you also are to love one another. By this all people will know that you are my disciples, if you have love for one another."* (John 13:34-35 ESV)

If you are still unclear, ask God daily to reveal Himself to you. Get on your knees and surrender completely your life to Him. Don't wait. Don't let your pride get in the way. Your relationship with Jesus is too important.

CHAPTER 13

DISCIPLINE

"For the moment all discipline seems painful rather than pleasant, but later it yields the peaceful fruit of righteousness to those who have been trained by it."
Hebrews 12:11 ESV

If you have lived a life that is more on the easy-believism, rather than Lordship salvation side, it may be good to do a detailed audit of your own salvation. You may be saved, but have been under poor teaching. It is time to put off the childish things and grow into what Jesus desires of you. There are several ways to check to see if you are of the faith. One very clear way of knowing if the Holy Spirit is inside you and that you are truly saved is through God's discipline.

Discipline is hard. When a child that is not my own does something wrong, I don't discipline him. If my own child does something wrong, you had better bet that I discipline him. Discipline is for my child's own good. I want him to succeed, so in my love for him I must discipline him.

The same is true for you and God if you are His child. He will surely discipline you while possibly not others around you who are not saved. When a true Christian breaks the law by cheating on their taxes, God will possibly allow an audit, or some other trial that is usually obvious as His discipline. I remember being upset with God and throwing a child-like tantrum. I had intended to read my Bible, but because I was mad, I decided to watch TV instead. God slammed me to the ground and hit me with the flu keeping me from going to multiple social gatherings I was looking forward to. Some might pass that off as life, but I knew it was clear discipline. My arrogant, do-it-my-own-way mentality had served me so well in my previous life, but now it gets me a firm slap of humility. I stumble and trip in areas I used to glide through with ease, all because God loves me and desires my growth. God's discipline can be seen and felt in many ways.

The beauty of discipline is in the fact that I know I am His. It is confirmation that I am a child of God and that I am truly saved. It also is a confirmation to my own child that he is mine and that I love him. While being disciplined is hard, he knows it is a form of love. My discipline is correcting him so that he does not end up in a worse place down the line. I explained it like this to my son when he was about five years old:

"Consider what will happen if you disobey simple instructions from me or if you lie to me. I am your mom so you will get disciplined. You may get a toy taken away, or put in a time-out, or you might even get a spanking if I feel it is necessary. I love you and want you to grow up to respect others and have others respect you. Ultimately, though, I want you to respect God.

"I want you to tell me, what would happen if you hit me? What would happen if you punched your dad in the face? What about your teacher? What if you hit a police officer in the face? How about the president or a king? With each level of authority the consequences are bigger, right?

"When I was a professional photographer I got to photograph one of our past presidents. Did you know that? Yep, it was pretty cool. They had to do a full background check on me and then, once I passed, I was given a special pin to wear on my lapel. Do you know what that pin did for me? It protected my life! It told the body guards that I was okay to come near the president. If I did not have that pin on, and I got too close to him, guess what would happen? I would get shot! If you punched the president in the face you would get shot. What do you think would happen if you punched God in the face? Wow, right? He could, in an instant, make you dust.

"If you continue down the path you are taking of disobedience with me, that will lead to maybe one day disobeying your teacher. The more you get away with things, the easier you think it is. The most loving thing I can do for you now, as my child, is discipline you. Not tomorrow, not some day, but today, right when you disobey. Do you want to be homeless? Of course not. Do you know what it means to be homeless? It means sleeping on the dirt, out in the cold, with the bugs and coyotes. It means not having any food or really any friends. It means being separated from me and your dad.

"Did you know that my disciplining you now is keeping you from being homeless? Yep! Think it through. If you disobey me and I allow it, you will then go on to disobey your teachers. Some may not tolerate it, but others will because they will be too tired to bother. You may just barely pass school and hopefully you will get a job. When you get a job, you will one day disobey your boss because you learned growing up that authority did not matter that much, and you like doing things your way. Do you know what disobeying your boss means? It means you get fired. You won't be able to get another job because your last boss won't give any recommendations for you. You will then end up without a job, with no money, and you will be homeless. How does that sound? Now do you understand why my disciplining you now is the most loving thing I can do?"

This story that I told my son when he was a child, I only had to tell him once. Every now and then I would remind him that I am disciplining him so he won't end up homeless and he got it. He knew that it was out of my great love for him that I disciplined him. He still gets this as a young man.

Let me share a story of how God disciplined me using my own child. As I just shared, I want to help my son grow up to respect authority. We live in a democracy where we get to vote, but when we are in heaven, there is no democracy, no vote. It is all God. Full-blown monarchy. Learning to submit to authority can be hard for many of us, and I try to remind myself that submission in heaven is non-negotiable.

I'm one of those people who have problems with authority. So much so that I have to verbally confirm, whenever I can, that if I place myself under someone's authority, I must submit to them. I remind myself that I fully understand that God will judge that person on how well they lead me, and I will be judged on how well I obey the person leading whether that person is right or wrong.

When we place ourselves under leadership, we hope and pray that they will lead us correctly, but in the end, there will be some things that they do wrong. Interestingly, we will not be responsible for their leading, just our obeying. So, after multiple conversations about this with several people in my life recently, it happened. I led someone wrong. In one specific area of my life, God has allowed me to have a major form of leadership for a short time with one person: I am a mom to a bright little boy. I would like to tell you a story about a time when I messed up.

One day, in late September of 2015, my son got an upset stomach. It was some sort of bug, and I found him in his room rather upset. He was seven at the time. We chatted about it and he said it was going away. I asked him if he prayed about it and he told me yes, that he told God he would not play his video games all day tomorrow if God would make his tummy feel better.

"TEACHING MOMENT" bannered across my mind.

I told him that is a bad place to put God. God is not a genie in a bottle waiting to be bargained with. He is GOD. We got on a great conversation about how big God is and how potentially bad it is to get in the habit of bargaining with the Almighty Creator of the Universe. He got it. He began to cry. He began to pray for forgiveness. We talked some more and I was able to tell him it is okay, he did not know, and God knew I would be here to teach him the right way. It was a great teaching moment. I shared with him that God not only loves him, but that He LIKES him too. God knows we are dust and knows we need His guidance and patience.

Fast forward to my son coming home from school the next afternoon and he instantly asked if he could go back on his vow and please could he play his video game. I told him absolutely not. Two hours later, I am trying to get work done and he is in typical "bored out of his mind because he can't do what he wants" mode. I have an appointment that should only last 30 minutes so I tell him, okay, go ahead and play the video game. I will allow it.

BIG MISTAKE. He plays his game. I get my work done. After 30 minutes I take him to the pool. We talk. I ask him how he felt playing his game. He said, not great. I told him that is his conscience bearing witness against him. He says, "Yes, mom, but you are the one at fault." Remember, I told you this is a story about my "bright" son. He is often the one teaching me the lesson. I ask him how it is that I am at fault. He said simply, "Because you are my mom and you said I could play."

HE NAILED IT! He was right. I can't remember, but I like to think I said I was sorry. Honestly I don't think I did because I was speechless. We went on with our evening. He went to bed, my husband went off to work for his night-shift job, and I decided to do something to help the ear problems I had been having by putting a drop of essential oil on and around my ear. I had been applying essential oils on and around my ears for months trying to work out the ringing I had. For some reason, on this night, the essential oil dripped into my ear canal on both sides.

I was swiftly given a heaping serving of pain like I have never felt before. It was worse than childbirth and I did that without any pain killers, fully natural. That was hard. This was about 10 times harder. I felt like someone was sticking literal knives into my skull and slightly turning them. The reason this pain was so bad was because there was no relief.

The initial pain lasted for four and a half hours with me crying so loud I'm surprised my neighbors did not call the cops thinking I was being beaten. At the four and a half hour mark, I was able to stop crying in agony, and the pain sort of subsided, but only in that I could sit still clenching my teeth for another hour, at which point I finally fell asleep for a bit sitting upright only to be woken up by the pain again.

A lot goes on in your mind when you are in that much writhing pain without any relief. I have never EVER gone through anything like that. To say I got a good look at my sin is an understatement. Let me walk you through my journey. About two hours in, crying my eyes out, or more like screaming in utter pain, I start to realize God is trying to teach me something bigger here. What?

When you are in that much pain it is hard to think about anything else. So I turn on my audio Bible and listen. Through my sobs and screams, rocking back and forth, I try to listen to some daily Bible readings on my phone: Isaiah 13-18. There it is. A small part of a verse tucked in Isaiah 17:11. "…in a day of grief and incurable pain."

My mind went to all of those people in my life who will potentially end up on the other side of eternity gnashing their teeth, writhing in incurable pain, and with more grief than they have ever known. Forever and ever. What a picture. What incredible sorrow I felt. Then my mind raced to Jesus. Six hours! SIX. LONG. HOURS. He endured pain on the cross. Not just any pain. The worst kind of pain; a pain that I am sure did not compare to mine.

It was then that I did the math. I knew, just *knew* God was going to make this thing last for six hours. I can't tell you how I knew, but I did. It was exactly six hours of pain that

God disciplined me with. I was humbled to say the least. My mind became clear and I knew what I had done wrong. YOU, my dear reader, know what I did wrong.

I was given one leadership job: my son. And I failed. I broke my son's vow to God. I had caused one of the least of these to sin. I deserved every ounce of pain plus more. I was horrified. I took my licks. I woke my son up in the morning and apologized. I learned my lesson. I was a bad steward of the "talent" God had given me. My son is one of my "talents" and my job is to grow him. My selfish world got in the way of upholding something I tried to teach him that was of the utmost importance: God. Then I tossed God aside for just a second. For what? For a stupid worldly appointment. For worldly peace and quiet so I could get my work done.

My world has shifted. It is the hard things in life that help us grow. I hope to never have to endure the kind of pain I experienced that night, but I also would never trade the experience for anything. The lessons I learned were priceless. I became resolved to endure whatever I need to for the sake of growth and the sake of loving and following Jesus. Nothing else matters. He matters. I resolve to stop messing around and be a better mom, a better wife, a better friend, a better servant, a better slave to Christ.

The discipline of God is real and palpable. When God chooses you and you respond correctly by giving your life to Him, your life here on this earth will not get easier, nor will it stay the same, but you will know, with certainty, that you are His because He will love you enough to discipline you. This discipline will sharpen you and mold you into the person God wants and desires you to be. It will strengthen you and allow you the honor of moving one step closer to Jesus. To be like Jesus and to be a blessing to God is at the heart of every Christian.

My life is all for the glory of God, and as a true Christian I deeply desire the glory of God. It is only through His mercy and grace that I am guaranteed, through the sealing of the Holy Spirit, an inheritance that I honestly can't even imagine. The angels in heaven must look at us sometimes in wonder. I can imagine them shaking their heads and saying to each other "if they only knew the half of it, they would obey without question."

CHAPTER 14

MERCY AND GRACE

"Let us then with confidence
draw near to the throne of grace,
that we may receive mercy and find grace
to help in time of need."
Hebrews 4:16 ESV

When Jacob was in grade school, at the age of eight, he got to experience first hand what mercy and grace meant. It was a summer afternoon and he was out roaming the neighborhood with several of the local kids in the community. They had been friends for a while and liked to explore and generally get into low-grade trouble as kids do. I needed him to come home, so I walked outside to find him. As I was calling his name while walking down the path by our community pool, I heard a noise just above me. I looked up, and to my shock and horror there were the kids, up on the roof of the bathroom building for the pool.

To give you some perspective, I am a mom who has always given my child a long leash. Normally I would have firmly told him to get down and then talked to him about the dangers of what he had done. He was eight, and I was confident in his climbing skills, but I would have wanted him to understand the potential for damaging public property and the simple fact that he could have fallen too for any number of reasons, and that this is precisely why there are community rules against climbing on the roof of the pool bathrooms.

While I wish this was all that happened, it was not what shocked me and filled me with horror at that moment. It was the fact that the older boys allowed the youngest boy, who was only four, to climb up there with them. I ordered them all down at once, in the firmest mom voice I could muster up, and then brought all of them over to sit on the stairs of our front porch. Once seated with their full attention, I let them all have it.

I had been a teacher for many years, so calmly guilt-tripping children into understanding and agreeing with my point was something I was highly skilled at. As I explained to them the error of their ways, the look on their faces told me they understood and were sorry for their actions. The four-year-old could have been killed and they all would have to live with that burden of fault in their hearts forever. They understood it was their responsibility to look after each other and make better choices based on the group rather than their own personal desires.

I told them all to go home, and they all fled like little birds fluttering off into the wind. Seated still, with eyes locked on me, was my own son. He was devastated. He knew there would be more because he was my child and we had been here before. Discipline. It was coming.

I sat down beside him and put my arm around him. I knew he was sorry. He looked up at me with tears in his eyes and whispered again, "I'm sorry mama." What a blessing that child is to me, even to this day. I gave him a hug and told him he was forgiven. I said, "Let's go inside, wash up, and I would like to take you out for ice cream."

The look of shock on his face was priceless. Instead of punishment, he was getting mercy, and instead of discipline, he was getting a reward? How could this be? As we drove to the ice cream shop, I shared with my son what mercy and grace mean. Mercy is not getting punished for something you deserve. Grace is getting something wonderful that you don't deserve.

Instead of punishment, I forgave him, and gave him a reward. This is counter to how we normally operate. It is counter to how any of us understand how the world works. You do something wrong, you should get punished, not rewarded. That's the beauty of God's mercy and grace. It doesn't make much sense to us humans, but when we experience it first-hand, it is the most wonderful blessing anyone can have.

My son was truly repentant. He fully knew what he had done wrong and he was deeply sorry for it. I could see that plainly. His sad demeanor and downtrodden face, along with his verbal apology was all I needed to know he was truly repentant. Showing him mercy and grace at that moment was, in my opinion, a good place to give him a glimpse of God's great mercy and grace that He has for His children.

"Steadfast love and faithfulness meet; righteousness and peace kiss each other." Psalm 85:10 (ESV)

The Hebrew word for "steadfast love" is "checed." Checed is translated most often as "mercy." The word for "faithfulness" is "'emeth" which is most often translated as "truth," but means firm reliability. This, to me is a picture of the stability and reliableness of the mercy of God. "Righteousness" or the Hebrew "tsedeq" means what is right or just and "peace" is Hebrew "shalowm" which has a meaning of completeness of welfare as it pertains to the covenant relationship with God.

Psalm 85:10 comes alive as I consider how poetic and true it is. God's mercy is firm and I can trust it, while His grace in completing and restoring myself back to Him is mind-blowing. When God's need for justice kisses His redemption plan, you get Jesus. Only Jesus. I deserve nothing, yet He loves me so deeply to bless me with His mercy and allow me the honor of receiving His grace which is everlasting life with Jesus.

There is an amazing sense of gratitude that comes over me when I think about God's mercy and grace in light of His glory. I remember getting into an argument with my husband early on in our marriage, and about six months after my salvation. I cannot remember what the argument was, but I do remember it was in front of our child, and I felt shattered. My husband had put me down. It felt mean to me and my pride was hurt. I am sure it wasn't mean at all, but living with someone who is very black and white about things, means oftentimes his words can cut to my core.

I was fuming mad, but I kept my mouth shut. I heard the Holy Spirit urging me to keep quiet and walk away. As calmly as I could, I turned around and went upstairs. I remember clear as day, with each step I took up the stairs, my heart softened. The Holy Spirit was calming me and impressing on me one very odd, yet clear request. I was mad, but all I could hear, over and over in my mind was, "Serve him. Bless him. Honor him."

Seriously, God? Serve him? Bless him? Honor Him?

After what my husband did, it was not something I felt like doing, but one thing I had learned in these early months after my conversion was that I needed to obey right away. I got to the top of the stairs and I was broken. I knew my husband was just a man. I needed to serve, bless, and honor him. I went into our bedroom and fully cleaned his side of the room. To this day, I do not even know if my husband noticed what I had done, but that was not the point. The point was that I obeyed God.

The moment that I let go of my anger and wrath toward someone who had wronged me, was the moment I felt an overwhelming sense of love from my Father. He was pleased, and I can tell you that I experienced a speck of His glory that day, and guess what, it was magical!

Do you get it now? This *is* the point. While this entire book, up until now, may have seemed heavy and burdensome, it was placed on my heart to start with the hard truths, so that the incredible glory of this awe-inspiring truth of mercy and grace would have the greatest impact. It is God's greatest impact on a fallen world.

As I read various authors who have written about the glory of God, I am always brought back to His mercy and grace. There are so many things in this world that give us a glimpse into God's glory. They are the things that make our hearts sing. Think about how we scream wildly at our children's sporting games in an effort to cheer them on. The kid who scores the winning point gets all the glory from his or her teammates who lift them onto their shoulders while cheering.

I remember traveling to Hawaii with my family and witnessing night after night the most gorgeous sunsets I have ever laid eyes on. Droves of people would come out every evening to witness the glory of each sunset.

When we go to Disneyland we watch the fireworks show in awe as their displays are the best around. The glory of their light-show in the air is splendid and hardly a head in the crowd is not turned to it.

We were built by God to acknowledge glory. I wonder if these little glories we experience on this earth are but a small glimpse into what it will most likely be like when we see God in all His glory. As I image what it might be like, I feel like these lesser glories I experience are like small fragments that have been afforded to us this side of heaven. Something tells me that the weight of His full glory would be too much for me to bear. It would overwhelm my human senses.

Oh what a day that will be, though! Can you imagine it? Everything in which we find wonder, excitement, joy, and glory here in this life, will be magnified to a limitless degree when we encounter the full glory of God. His mercy and grace have guaranteed it!

....

PART 3

....

THE TOOLS

CHAPTER 15

FRUITS AND TESTIMONY

"You will recognize them by their fruits."
Matthew 7:16 ESV

There are at least 22 specific areas that you can use to audit your salvation. This is not an exhaustive list of finding proof of salvation, and your salvation is something between you and God, but this list can be a helpful tool for you to discover areas of your life where you may be weak and possibly areas in which you have been erroneous. In the words of Paul to the Colossians, this is my prayer also:

"And so, from the day we heard, we have not ceased to pray for you, asking that you may be filled with the knowledge of his will in all spiritual wisdom and understanding, so as to walk in a manner worthy of the Lord, fully pleasing to him: bearing fruit in every good work and increasing in the knowledge of God; being strengthened with all power, according to his glorious might, for all endurance and patience with joy; giving thanks to the Father, who has qualified you to share in the inheritance of the saints in light." (Colossians 1:9-12 ESV)

Audit #1:

Is your character in keeping with the Fruit of the Spirit?
Galatians 5:22-23 ESV

> *"But the fruit of the Spirit is love, joy, peace, patience, kindness, goodness, faithfulness, gentleness, self-control; against such things there is no law."*

Audit #2:

Is your life defined by the Spirit or the flesh?
Galatians 5:16-26 ESV

> *"But I say, walk by the Spirit, and you will not gratify the desires of the flesh. For the desires of the flesh are against the Spirit, and the desires of the Spirit are against the flesh, for these are opposed to each other, to keep you from doing the things you want to do. But if you are led by the Spirit, you are not under the law. Now the works of the flesh are evident: sexual immorality, impurity, sensuality, idolatry, sorcery, enmity, strife, jealousy, fits of anger, rivalries, dissensions, divisions, envy, drunkenness, orgies, and things like these. I warn you, as I warned you before, that those who do such things will not inherit the kingdom of God. But the fruit of the Spirit is love, joy, peace, patience, kindness, goodness, faithfulness, gentleness, self-control; against such things there is no law. And those who belong to Christ Jesus have crucified the flesh with its passions and desires. If we live by the Spirit, let us also keep in step with the Spirit. Let us not become conceited, provoking one another, envying one another."*

Audit #3:

Do you actively make disciples?
Matthew 28:19 ESV

> *"Go therefore and make disciples of all nations, baptizing them in the name of the Father and of the Son and of the Holy Spirit,"*

Audit #4:

Do you love God with all that you are?

Matthew 22:37-38 ESV

> "And he said to him, "You shall love the Lord your God with all your heart and with all your soul and with all your mind. This is the great and first commandment."

Audit #5:

Do you crave the Word of God?

1 Peter 2:2-3 ESV

> "Like newborn infants, long for the pure spiritual milk, that by it you may grow up into salvation— if indeed you have tasted that the Lord is good."

Romans 7:22 ESV

> "For I delight in the law of God, in my inner being,"

Matthew 5:6 ESV

> "Blessed are those who hunger and thirst for righteousness, for they shall be satisfied."

Audit #6: Do you keep His commands?

Exodus 20:3-17 ESV

> 3 "You shall have no other gods before me.
>
> 4 "You shall not make for yourself a carved image, or any likeness of anything that is in heaven above, or that is in the earth beneath, or that is in the water under the earth. 5 You shall not bow down to them or serve them, for I the Lord your God am a jealous God, visiting the iniquity of the fathers on the children to the third and the fourth generation of those who hate me, 6 but showing steadfast love to thousands of those who love me and keep my commandments.
>
> 7 "You shall not take the name of the Lord your God in vain, for the Lord will not hold him guiltless who takes his name in vain.

[8] *"Remember the Sabbath day, to keep it holy.* [9] *Six days you shall labor, and do all your work,* [10] *but the seventh day is a Sabbath to the Lord your God. On it you shall not do any work, you, or your son, or your daughter, your male servant, or your female servant, or your livestock, or the sojourner who is within your gates.* [11] *For in six days the Lord made heaven and earth, the sea, and all that is in them, and rested on the seventh day. Therefore the Lord blessed the Sabbath day and made it holy.*

[12] *"Honor your father and your mother, that your days may be long in the land that the Lord your God is giving you.*

[13] *"You shall not murder.*

[14] *"You shall not commit adultery.*

[15] *"You shall not steal.*

[16] *"You shall not bear false witness against your neighbor.*

[17] *"You shall not covet your neighbor's house; you shall not covet your neighbor's wife, or his male servant, or his female servant, or his ox, or his donkey, or anything that is your neighbor's."*

Audit #7:

Is God's Law written on your heart?

Jeremiah 31:33 ESV

> *"For this is the covenant that I will make with the house of Israel after those days, declares the Lord: I will put my law within them, and I will write it on their hearts. And I will be their God, and they shall be my people."*

Hebrews 10:14-16 ESV

> *"For by a single offering he has perfected for all time those who are being sanctified. And the Holy Spirit also bears witness to us; for after saying, "This is the covenant that I will make with them after those days, declares the Lord: I will put my laws on their hearts, and write them on their minds,"*

Audit #8:
Do you grow in God's wisdom or human knowledge?
James 1:5 ESV
> *"If any of you lacks wisdom, let him ask God, who gives generously to all without reproach, and it will be given him."*

Colossians 1:9 ESV
> *"And so, from the day we heard, we have not ceased to pray for you, asking that you may be filled with the knowledge of his will in all spiritual wisdom and understanding,"*

Audit #9:
Do you love others?
1 John 4:7-12 ESV
> *"Beloved, let us love one another, for love is from God, and whoever loves has been born of God and knows God. Anyone who does not love does not know God, because God is love. In this the love of God was made manifest among us, that God sent his only Son into the world, so that we might live through him. In this is love, not that we have loved God but that he loved us and sent his Son to be the propitiation for our sins. Beloved, if God so loved us, we also ought to love one another. No one has ever seen God; if we love one another, God abides in us and his love is perfected in us."*

Audit #10:
Do you love your enemy?
1 Corinthians 4:12 ESV
> *"and we labor, working with our own hands. When reviled, we bless; when persecuted, we endure;"*

Matthew 5:43-46 ESV
> *"You have heard that it was said, 'You shall love your neighbor and hate your enemy.' But I say to you, Love your enemies and*

pray for those who persecute you, so that you may be sons of your Father who is in heaven. For he makes his sun rise on the evil and on the good, and sends rain on the just and on the unjust. For if you love those who love you, what reward do you have? Do not even the tax collectors do the same?"

Audit #11:

Do you have too much love for the things of this world?
1 John 2:15-17 ESV

"Do not love the world or the things in the world. If anyone loves the world, the love of the Father is not in him. For all that is in the world—the desires of the flesh and the desires of the eyes and pride of life—is not from the Father but is from the world. And the world is passing away along with its desires, but whoever does the will of God abides forever."

John 15:19 ESV

"If you were of the world, the world would love you as its own; but because you are not of the world, but I chose you out of the world, therefore the world hates you."

Audit #12:

Are you politically correct when it comes to Jesus when you are with your friends, family, and coworkers?
Matthew 10:32-33 ESV

"So everyone who acknowledges me before men, I also will acknowledge before my Father who is in heaven, but whoever denies me before men, I also will deny before my Father who is in heaven."

Audit #13:

Do you have chronic sin?
1 John 3:6-10 ESV

"No one who abides in him keeps on sinning; no one who keeps on sinning has either seen him or known him. Little children, let no one deceive you. Whoever practices righteousness is

righteous, as he is righteous. Whoever makes a practice of sinning is of the devil, for the devil has been sinning from the beginning. The reason the Son of God appeared was to destroy the works of the devil. No one born of God makes a practice of sinning, for God's seed abides in him; and he cannot keep on sinning, because he has been born of God. By this it is evident who are the children of God, and who are the children of the devil: whoever does not practice righteousness is not of God, nor is the one who does not love his brother."

Audit #14:

Do you get disciplined by God?

Hebrews 12:5b-11 ESV

> *"My son, do not regard lightly the discipline of the Lord, nor be weary when reproved by him. For the Lord disciplines the one he loves, and chastises every son whom he receives."*
>
> *"It is for discipline that you have to endure. God is treating you as sons. For what son is there whom his father does not discipline? If you are left without discipline, in which all have participated, then you are illegitimate children and not sons. Besides this, we have had earthly fathers who disciplined us and we respected them. Shall we not much more be subject to the Father of spirits and live? For they disciplined us for a short time as it seemed best to them, but he disciplines us for our good, that we may share his holiness. For the moment all discipline seems painful rather than pleasant, but later it yields the peaceful fruit of righteousness to those who have been trained by it."*

Audit #15:

Do you get tested by God?

James 1:2-3 ESV

> *"Count it all joy, my brothers, when you meet trials of various kinds, for you know that the testing of your faith produces steadfastness."*

1 Peter 4:12-13 ESV

"Beloved, do not be surprised at the fiery trial when it comes upon you to test you, as though something strange were happening to you. But rejoice insofar as you share Christ's sufferings, that you may also rejoice and be glad when his glory is revealed."

Audit #16:

Are you convicted when you sin?

John 16:7-11 ESV (note: the Helper is the Holy Spirit)

"Nevertheless, I tell you the truth: it is to your advantage that I go away, for if I do not go away, the Helper will not come to you. But if I go, I will send him to you. And when he comes, he will convict the world concerning sin and righteousness and judgment: concerning sin, because they do not believe in me; concerning righteousness, because I go to the Father, and you will see me no longer; concerning judgment, because the ruler of this world is judged."

Audit #17:

Do you get persecuted for your faith?

2 Timothy 3:12 ESV

"Indeed, all who desire to live a godly life in Christ Jesus will be persecuted,"

Matthew 5:10 ESV

"Blessed are those who are persecuted for righteousness' sake, for theirs is the kingdom of heaven."

John 15:18 ESV

"If the world hates you, know that it has hated me before it hated you."

1 Peter 3:14 ESV

"But even if you should suffer for righteousness' sake, you will be blessed. Have no fear of them, nor be troubled,"

1 Peter 4:14 ESV

"If you are insulted for the name of Christ, you are blessed, because the Spirit of glory and of God rests upon you."

Audit #18:

Are you hated by some people because of your faith?

1 John 3:13 ESV

"Do not be surprised, brothers, that the world hates you."

Luke 6:22 ESV

"Blessed are you when people hate you and when they exclude you and revile you and spurn your name as evil, on account of the Son of Man!"

Audit #19:

Do you see a changed life in yourself?

Ezekiel 36:25-26 ESV

"I will sprinkle clean water on you, and you shall be clean from all your uncleannesses, and from all your idols I will cleanse you. And I will give you a new heart, and a new spirit I will put within you. And I will remove the heart of stone from your flesh and give you a heart of flesh."

2 Corinthians 5:17 ESV

"Therefore, if anyone is in Christ, he is a new creation. The old has passed away; behold, the new has come."

Audit #20:

Has your spiritual life grown and changed since last year?

Colossians 1:10 ESV

"so as to walk in a manner worthy of the Lord, fully pleasing to him: bearing fruit in every good work and increasing in the knowledge of God;"

2 Peter 3:18 ESV
"But grow in the grace and knowledge of our Lord and Savior Jesus Christ. To him be the glory both now and to the day of eternity. Amen."

Audit #21:

Christian: Would a stranger or even a close friend or family member who is not a follower of Christ convict you in a court of law of being a Christian?

1 John 5:19 ESV
"We know that we are from God, and the whole world lies in the power of the evil one."

Colossians 4:5-6 ESV
"Walk in wisdom toward outsiders, making the best use of the time. Let your speech always be gracious, seasoned with salt, so that you may know how you ought to answer each person."

1 Corinthians 1:21-23 ESV
"For since, in the wisdom of God, the world did not know God through wisdom, it pleased God through the folly of what we preach to save those who believe. For Jews demand signs and Greeks seek wisdom, but we preach Christ crucified, a stumbling block to Jews and folly to Gentiles,"

Audit #22:

Do you find assurance or conviction when you read the entire book of 1 John?

Take some time to really consider the audits in this chapter. Work through them one at a time, and then move onto writing out your personal testimony. Your fruits will become a part of your testimony.

Your Testimony

Once you complete an audit on your personal growth and fruit, consider writing out your own personal testimony using the following guidelines. God's desire is for the salvation of His people. We must start with God's grace and mercy and know our conversion is true before we embark upon discovering the truths and promises that are specifically for God's people. Prayerfully ask God to open your heart and your mind to see how your story is unfolding. Think of a time when you fully understood the gospel. It would have been a time that the Holy Spirit was convincing you of your sin in a way that felt crushing. It would have been a time when you felt utterly guilty of your sin. It would have been a time that you felt like the scales over your eyes were torn off, you fully understood the weight of your sin, and what it meant to follow Jesus.

Some people may have a mental block because they cannot get past the time when they were a child. They feel proud that they were "saved" at a young age or that they were saved because of some altar call or sinner's prayer they prayed. I encourage you to consider that may not be your actual salvation point. It is not a huge issue if you are saved now and you still consider your salvation point when you were five, or when you prayed the prayer, but do realize, placing God on His knees in submission to your whim may not be when you were saved.

Can you think of a time in your life that you felt the burden of the Holy Spirit pressing on you? Perhaps that time is now. Perhaps that time was in college. Perhaps you were a young child who was wise beyond your years. God does the impossible, so in reality, any age of salvation is absolutely perfect, because God is perfect. The point of this exercise is to describe when you felt like the Holy Spirit truly got a hold of your heart and convicted you of your sin, your need to be holy, and an understanding of your pending judgment before a holy God.

Take some time to write out your story by answering the following questions. Use a journal or use the space provided in the separate Study Guide.

1. How was the Holy Spirit working on you before your actual conversion? What do you remember about Him convincing you that you are a sinner? What was it like when you needed to confess your sins and turn from them to follow Jesus?

2. What specific sins were revealed to you that convinced you of your sin and need to repent?

3. When did you give your life to the lordship of Jesus and what did that look like? (If you cannot pinpoint a specific date or time, a season of your life may be all you remember.)

4. How did your life change after your conversion?

5. What fruits and growth have you seen in your life since your conversion? (See Fruits Audit)

CHAPTER 16

HOW TO READ THE BIBLE

"This Book of the Law shall not depart from your mouth, but you shall meditate on it day and night, so that you may be careful to do according to all that is written in it. For then you will make your way prosperous, and then you will have good success."
Joshua 1:8 ESV

I recommend that you read the entire Bible, cover to cover, as often as you can. It is the greatest way to guard yourself against heresy (faulty beliefs about God that are not true). If you are new to reading God's Word, rather than starting at the beginning of the Book, I have outlined a slightly different approach. Once you get through the first approach, come back every year and make a point to read the entire Bible in one year.

There are several apps and programs you can use for daily Bible reading that will keep you on track, giving you some Old Testament and some New Testament readings every day. I like using the YouVersion app for this. It only takes around 71 hours to read through the entire Bible. If you spend just 12 minutes per day reading, you will read the entire Bible in 365 days! You can even set the YouVersion app to wake you up at a certain time every morning and prompt you right where you left off. Wake up, read for 12 minutes, then start your day. You may even want to come back to the daily reading at night to go over it a second time before bed.

When an orchestra tunes their instruments, they do it before the performance, not after. It is why I recommend reading before you start your day. If you want to read at night, that is great too, but always try to read in the morning first so that your mind is set on the things above before the craziness of the day sets in.

Background of the Bible

The Bible is a series of letters and manuscripts from various authors beginning many centuries before Jesus' birth and ending about fifty years after his death. It is an account of the foundation and early church history along with predictive prophecy of what is to come in our future.

There are 66 books in the Protestant Bible. There are 39 Hebrew-Aramaic books in the Old Testament from Genesis to Malachi and 27 books in the New Testament from Matthew to Revelation. The Torah is the first five books in the Bible and are what are referred to as the "Pentateuch" or the "Five Books of Moses" since many theologians consider him to be the author. The Torah is often the name used when speaking of Jewish teachings. The Catholic Bible has seven additional books that are called the "Apocrypha." The Protestant Bibles do not contain these for a variety of reasons, including issues of unknown authorship or questionable internal inconsistencies.

You will see the Bible broken up into books, chapters, and verses. These were not there in the original text, but are helpful for us today as we read and note various locations. While many think you should start at the beginning of any book, the Bible is a little different. It is best to look at each of the 66 books of the Bible as individual books that inform and help reveal the entire story of God's plan.

How to start reading the Bible

If you are new to Christianity or new to reading the Bible, I recommended that you start with the book of John. It is found in the New Testament in the last half of the book. John is the fourth gospel. Feel free to go back to the beginning of the New Testament to get a good understanding of who Jesus is. The books of Matthew, Mark, and Luke are considered the Synoptic Gospel messages of the life of Jesus according to that specific person's perspective. They are synoptic, because they contain many of the same stories.

Starting with John will give you a good understanding of who Jesus is. Once you finish John, skip over to Romans, a couple of books later. Romans is helpful to understand the gospel message and doctrine (what Christian beliefs are.) Then read James, which will help you gain an understanding for the life of a Christian. Along the way feel free to mix in Psalms and Proverbs as they are very uplifting and encouraging. You will find those two books almost right in the very middle of the Bible.

Once you have a good understanding of Jesus and the gospel message, head to the beginning of the book at Genesis. Jesus was there at the beginning (although not called out by name) so it is exciting to read it with that truth already in your understanding of the story. Read John chapter 1 alongside Genesis to see Jesus in Genesis. Feel free to read through Exodus if you want to get a good understanding of Moses. Then go back to the New Testament and start reading through all of the gospels: Matthew, Mark, Luke, and John again.

Then simply continue reading through the Bible to the end. After John, keep going with Acts, then all of the letters, starting with 1 Corinthians. Every time you get to the beginning of the next book, read the introduction so you understand who wrote it and to whom it was written. If you do not see an introduction in your Bible, consider getting a study Bible or a good Bible commentary. You may also use free online resources as a tool to find out the background of each book. As you read, consider the context in which it was written, to whom it was written, and why. Ask yourself what it meant to the people then, what does it mean universally to all of us, and what does it mean to you now. This is called the Inductive Bible Study method. (See Chapter 17 for instructions)

Simple order to follow:

- John
- Romans
- James
- Psalms
- Proverbs
- Genesis
- Exodus

- Matthew
- Mark
- Luke
- John (again)
- Acts
- Romans (again)
- Then keep reading through to the end of the Bible, all the way through Revelation
- Sprinkle back in Psalms as it refreshes the soul
- Then go back and get into all of the Old Testament stories – they are quite incredible!

As you read through the Old Testament, it is helpful to use Bible commentaries to understand some of the context and meaning. After this first experience through the Bible, get started on a daily reading plan that takes you through in a year. The ESV Study Bible One Year Reading Plan is a good one and can be followed for free on the YouVersion Bible app available on iTunes and Google Play.

I hope this helps break things down a bit and lead you toward a viable plan to accomplish the goal of reading and understanding the Bible.

CHAPTER 17

BIBLE STUDY

*"All Scripture is breathed out by God
and profitable for teaching, for reproof, for correction,
and for training in righteousness, that the man of God
may be complete, equipped for every good work."*
2 Timothy 3:16-17 ESV

There are many resources available to help you study the Bible. Men and women have written helpful (and sometimes not so helpful) commentaries on the Bible. Finding a good commentary may seem hard, but I encourage you to consider using tools that are vetted by a larger group of people such as Ligonier Ministries. You can find which commentaries they recommend at: www.ligonier.org/blog/top-commentaries-on-every-book-of-the-bible

The Gospel Coalition is another great resource for good Bible based reading. They have a good resource on their website for recommended books: www.thegospelcoalition.org/recommended-books

Many "popular" studies can lead you astray, so be careful with mainstream works such as Jesus Calling. Here is a good article about that series to help you understand how easy it is to be led down a dangerous path when reading books that are not the Bible: www.challies.com/articles/10-serious-problems-with-jesus-calling

The best way to study the Bible is to simply study the Bible. Inductive study is a method that is easy to understand and can be applied right away as you are working through a book of the Bible. At its core, inductive study is considering the context of the verse or passage as it pertains to the entire Bible as a whole. There are several ways to approach inductive study and I have listed two ways below.

TRADITIONAL METHOD

The first is the traditional method. It uses three words to mark each area of study. **Observation** asks all of the questions regarding context. **Interpretation** asks how should it be interpreted based on the things that were observed. **Application** asks how we can apply what we have read to our own lives.

- Observation
- Interpretation
- Application

Observation (What does the text say?)

Ask the following questions:

1. Who wrote it?
2. Who was it written to or for?
3. Why was it written?
4. What is the goal or main message?
5. What did the writer hope to accomplish?
6. Where was it written?
7. Where was it received?
8. When was it written?

Interpretation (What does the text mean?)

1. How would the original hearer of the words interpret them?
2. What is the cultural context of the text?
3. What other passages in the Bible can be used to help interpret the one in question?

Application (What does the text mean to me?)

How should you, the reader of today, in the present, apply the verse or passage based on the understanding of the context and universal meaning?

CUP METHOD

The second inductive Bible study method is a way to help you remember each step using an acronym. The interpretation section of the traditional method is placed into the Context section and the Universal section is a place to understand the overarching meaning of the text by writing it out in your own words.

The intention for doing inductive study is to allow you to fill your cup when reading the Bible. I find so many people feel confused or say it is hard to understand the Bible. This method will allow you to really get to the heart of what God's message is. The CUP method of discovering the **Context**, and then determining what the **Universal** truth is, and finally applying that truth to your own life in your **Personal** response, allows the student to bring God's word to life in a whole new way.

- Context
- Universal
- Personal

Context

Ask the following questions:

1. Who wrote it and who was it written to or for?
2. Why was it written and what is the goal or main message?
3. Where was it written and where was it received?
4. When was it written?

5. How would the original hearer of the words interpret them?

6. What is the cultural context of the text?

7. What other passages in the Bible can be used to help interpret the one in question?

Universal
What is the universal truth of the verse or passage?

Personal
How should you, the reader of today, personally apply the verse or passage based on the understanding of the context and universal meaning?

An easy way to start Inductive Bible Study on your own is to look first at the context of the book you want to read. You may also consider getting a good commentary. Go to the link listed in the first part of this chapter at ligonier.org for a list of commentaries. It is also a good idea to check out various translations. I personally use the ESV (English Standard Version), which is a word-for-word translation. Some like to use the NIV (New International Version) or NLT (New Living Translation) as those are more thought-for-thought.

The KJV (King James Version) or NKJV (New King James Version) are a bit more difficult to read, but may be used as well. Many assume that the KJV is the only authorized Bible, but it is not. It is an okay translation, in my opinion, but I feel the ESV is the best for reading and understanding a word-for-word translation. All of these translations are translated from the first known early manuscripts. A good translation is never copied from another translation as some may assume.

When you notice translation differences, try looking up that verse using the Strong's Concordance. A free version of it may be used at www.blueletterbible.org and you may easily look up the verse, then select the TOOLS button to the left of the verse. It will open up a chart that gives you each word or phrase broken down. Just to the right of each phrase you will see a Strong's number that looks like G2532 (that is the number for the Greek word "and") or H853 (the number for the Hebrew word "and"). Click on that number and you will find a wealth of information to help you better understand the word and how/why it was used at the time it was written.

CHAPTER 18

PRAYER

....

"Rejoice always, pray without ceasing,
give thanks in all circumstances;
for this is the will of God in Christ Jesus for you."
1 Thessalonians 5:16-18

Once I became a Holy Spirit-filled Christian, prayer instantly become a major part of my life, just like filling your lungs with air and blinking your eyes. Some may assume it is something we are taught. While, yes, I did learn to pray growing up, when I actually become saved, it was automatic. It was no longer something I needed to work at. Before I was saved, I remember always trying to pray more, and working at it like a discipline. It was hard, but I assumed working at it was what we, as Christians, were to do.

When I became a Christian, at my true conversion, I found that I was praying all of the time. Randomly, I would catch myself talking to God in my thoughts. Every thought was held captive by the Holy Spirit that now dwelt in me. It was such a clear shift in my life that I started asking other Christians about it. What I found was interesting. Those who were years and years past their original salvation date would say, "Yes, of course I pray all of the time." Then they would qualify it with specific times like, in the morning, at mealtime, with family, at bedtime, etc. I even heard some saying it is hard to find time to pray, but they know it is important, or that it is something they are trying to work on. This felt normal to me, like what I experienced when I thought I was saved.

The really interesting part was when I asked the newer Christians. They all had the same response! They would say with passion, "YES! It is like I cannot turn it off! My mind is constantly chatting with Jesus all day long as if I cannot *not* talk with Him!" Why was there such a difference?

1 Thessalonians 5:19 (ESV) says, *"Do not quench the Spirit."* As I have grown in my walk with God, I have found that the more I try to do things on my own, the less I feel the Holy Spirit. Galatians 5:16 (ESV) says *"But I say, walk by the Spirit, and you will not gratify the desires of the flesh."* Then a little further down in Galatians 5:25 (ESV) *"If we live by the Spirit, let us also keep in step with the Spirit."*

While there are no specific Bible verses that talk about Christians losing their ability to pray over time, there are verses that let us know that we can very easily allow this world and our own desires to crowd out His still small voice. The phrase "still small voice" is from the King James Version of 1 Kings 19:12: *"And after the earthquake a fire; but the Lord was not in the fire: and after the fire a still small voice."* The Hebrew word for "still," is transliterated as *děmamah,* and means a whisper. The Hebrew word for "small," is transliterated as *daq,* and means small and thin, or almost crushed, like fine dust. This whisper that is like fine dust would potentially be easily missed if one doesn't carefully pay close attention. This is what I think happens to mature Christians who allow life to crowd out their internal dialogue with God. They may no longer hear it.

I also wonder if, like in raising our own children, God trains us to hear Him by not being so overtly loud as we move along in our sanctification. Like, perhaps, in the beginning, it will be clear, and as we mature, the voice becomes less obvious as we are to be trained up in righteousness. I remember distinctly feeling the pull of the Holy Spirit for me to pray many times in my early years as a new Christian. It was so clear, as if in my mind all I could hear was, "PRAY!" A few times I ignored the call only to realize within a minute my husband would come home or my child would come into the room demanding my attention. Ding, ding, ding! I got it loud and clear. When the Holy Spirit nudged me, God was training me to listen without delay.

One of my best friends, Tiffany, uses this catchy phrase with her kids that I feel fits here well. "Listen and obey, right away, all the way, with a happy heart." As I grow in Christ, He is not as obvious with me. He knows I already learned this lesson and He should not have to keep feeding me milk.

> *"For though by this time you ought to be teachers, you need someone to teach you again the basic principles of the oracles of God. You need milk, not solid food, for everyone who lives on milk is unskilled in the word of righteousness, since he is a child. But solid food is for the mature, for those who have their powers of discernment trained by constant practice to distinguish good from evil."* (Hebrews 5:12-14 ESV)

I diligently held His early lessons with me. Today, I can go through bouts of distracted prayerless hours, but when I am fully plugged into the Holy Spirit, prayer is an automatic part of my daily life. It has become a new thought process for me. If you are wanting this too, let's go back to the basics about what prayer is and how to retrain yourself to hear God's still small voice.

What is Prayer?

Prayer is the way we communicate with God. God lovingly desires our communion with Him on a daily basis. Scripture even encourages us to pray continuously and without ceasing. 1 Thessalonians 5:17 (ESV) says, *"Pray without ceasing."* This can be hard for the average person in today's media-swollen world. Our lives can be overwhelmingly full and increasingly busy, and prayer sometimes gets pushed off to the side or into a small portion of your morning or evening. We know from Scripture that prayer should be essential to the Christian walk. So what does it look like? When should it be done? Where should we pray? Should it be done on your knees? In a prayer closet? Should prayer be done in a journal?

There is no one right answer for any of these questions. Scripture has given us many, many examples of prayer, from late night, all night pour your heart out to God prayers, to going off for several days in the woods, to finding a quiet room alone, to praying with others gathered together in God's name. Prayer is also often seen in many of the letters written to the Churches. Prayer is a way for us to bless God, acknowledge Him, thank Him, and glorify Him, but it is also a way for us to love those around us. Outside of the vertical response to God and the horizontal outpouring with others, prayer is a way for us to confess our sins and gain clarity on God's will for our life and His church.

One of the most influential theological authors of the 20th century was A.W. Tozer. He wrote many beloved books such as *The Pursuit of God* and *The Knowledge of the Holy*, both of which all Christians should read. Tozer was born into a poor family and did not have any formal education, yet he is considered one of the most intelligent theologians who has been able to exposit the wondrous truths about God. It is said that when he dove deep into understanding these truths about God, he would get on his knees and pray... hard. He would ask God to reveal Himself to him and give him spiritual wisdom to understand the Bible.

Throughout the Bible, God tells us to ask for "wisdom." You might be interested to know that the way Hebrews understood the meaning of the word "wisdom" is not how we use the word today. "Chokmah" is the Hebrew and "sophia" is the Greek word that is translated as "wisdom."

The people of Israel knew that when learning from the Bible or when they were taught things of God, wisdom is what they needed to fully understand and appreciate the deeper meaning. Wisdom is the practical application of God's will through His Word. When we study the Bible, is it to gain greater understanding and greater knowledge? While knowledge and understanding of the Bible is a crucial part of the Christian walk, the more important factor is its practical life application of doing God's will rather than your own.

> "Orthodoxy, or right opinion, is, at best, a very slender part of religion. Though right tempers cannot subsist without right opinions, yet right opinions may subsist without right tempers. There may be a right opinion of God without either love or one right temper toward Him. Satan is a proof of this." – John Wesley

While I agree with Wesley's statement, for me it needs a bit more clarity. Orthodoxy or doctrine *is* an important part of religion, but insofar as to say it helps us define who God is and what He is saying to us. I believe Wesley's statement to mean doctrine is not the full picture in light of conversion. Satan and the demons agree with doctrine and they shutter.

Think of it this way: who are you the biggest expert on? You! At our core, we are all selfish, self-absorbed, egotistical, self-centered humans. But, when you fall in love and commit to another person, what happens? It becomes all about *them* and what *they* want (at least during the honeymoon stage). That is kind of how it is with God, only it is permanent. Once you are His, fully and unconditionally His, your understanding of the word "wisdom" will come to life. Your prayer life will change. Your motives for your life will change. YOU will change! How utterly exciting!

Rest in that blessing, and ask for wisdom... God's wisdom, not yours, or the wisdom of the world, but the wisdom of understanding God's will every single day. When you pray, just talk to God. Tell Him everything! Don't keep saying His name over and over again to fill the space... just talk. When I talk to my friend I don't keep inserting her name at every phrase or new thought. Do you? Pour your heart out and know that He hears you and delights in you.

If you appreciate easy ways to remember things, there are several different ways to approach prayer. Please remember, prayer is not a formula and not a box to be checked. The more you pray, the more you will desire to pray. The more we become a praying nation, praying with Kingdom eyes, the more the world will see the gospel in us. The love and light of Jesus will shine through you as you pray more earnestly and consistently to God.

A.C.T.S. Prayer Model

The following is a prayer model that is often used in Christian circles to help us cover important topics in prayer outside of only asking God to help us. It reminds us to pause first and praise Him, then ask Him for forgiveness, which naturally fills us with gratitude and thanksgiving, at which point we may ask (supplicate) for His help and guidance.

Adoration:

Adoration is a way to give glory to God. Many find it helpful to take one or two of God's attributes to meditate on during this portion of prayer. Simply thinking on how big God is can be a helpful tool to set your heart in the right spot for prayer. His incommunicable attributes are the characteristics of God that are only His such as His holiness (set apart and pure), omnipotence (all-powerful), omniscience (knows everything), omnipresence (is everywhere), immutability (unchangeable), and so on. See the next chapter on Attributes of God.

> *"Praise the Lord! Praise the name of the Lord, give praise, O servants of the Lord, who stand in the house of the Lord, in the courts of the house of our God! Praise the Lord, for the Lord is good; sing to his name, for it is pleasant!"* (Psalm 135:1-3 ESV)

Confession:

After you set yourself in the right mindset of coming before a Holy God, it is important to confess your sins and come clean. Confession and repentance is an important part of what it means to follow Jesus. Without confession and repentance (turning from our sin) there can be no true faith and trust in Jesus. Saying you are sorry to someone means nothing to them unless you mean it. It is the same way with God. He is not interested in our rote prayer of apologizing for something just to apologize. When you confess, consider your motives and the truth of the matter. Does your heart fully repent? Do you truly want forgiveness? Are you ready to turn away from your sins?

> *"Search me, O God, and know my heart! Try me and know my thoughts! And see if there be any grievous way in me, and lead me in the way everlasting!"* (Psalm 139:23-24 ESV)

> *"If we confess our sins, he is faithful and just to forgive us our sins and to cleanse us from all unrighteousness."* (1 John 1:9 ESV)

> *"Create in me a clean heart, O God, and renew a right spirit within me."* (Psalm 51:10 ESV)

Thanksgiving:
There is a natural transition of giving God thanks after we have confessed our sins and He has forgiven us. There should be an outpouring of gratitude toward the One who has delivered you from death. Use this time to humbly acknowledge what He has done for you, and allow the weight of that to sink in. The wondrous fact that He not only had mercy on you by removing your guilt, but also that He has given you grace by giving you more than you deserve in your salvation is enough to fill your heart and mind with thankfulness.

> *"I give thanks to you, O Lord my God, with my whole heart, and I will glorify your name forever."* (Psalm 86:12 ESV)

> *"I will give thanks to the Lord with my whole heart; I will recount all of your wonderful deeds. I will be glad and exult in you; I will sing praise to your name, O Most High."* (Psalm 9:1-2 ESV)

Supplication:

The word supplication means to ask. The connotation of the word can mean to beg or fall on your knees in humility. It is often why you hear people talking about praying on their knees. It is not necessary, but sometimes you will feel it is. You may even feel the need to lay prostrate (flat on your stomach, face down) on the floor before God.

While God asks us to come to Him with everything, by the time you get through the first three parts of the ACTS prayer method, your prayer requests may have changed. John 15:7 will make more sense once your view of God is raised high. When you abide in God, and His holy words in Scripture abide in you, anything you ask for will be aligned with God's will because you will desire only to pray for God's will.

"If you abide in me, and my words abide in you, ask whatever you wish, and it will be done for you." (John 15:7 ESV)

"You did not choose me, but I chose you and appointed you that you should go and bear fruit and that your fruit should abide, so that whatever you ask the Father in my name, he may give it to you." (John 15:16 ESV)

"Until now you have asked nothing in my name. Ask, and you will receive, that your joy may be full." (John 16:24 ESV)

"My help comes from the Lord, who made heaven and earth." (Psalm 121:2 ESV)

"Whatever you ask in my name, this I will do, that the Father may be glorified in the Son. If you ask me anything in my name, I will do it." (John 14:13-14 ESV)

The Lord's Prayer Model

"Pray then like this: 'Our Father in heaven, hallowed be your name. Your kingdom come, your will be done, on earth as it is in heaven. Give us this day our daily bread, and forgive us our debts, as we also have forgiven our debtors. And lead us not into temptation, but deliver us from evil.'" (Matthew 6:9-13 ESV)

Basic Outline

The basic outline below can help you categorize each part of the Lord's Prayer into seven specific areas of prayer.

1. God's due Praise
"Our Father in heaven, hallowed be your name."

2. God's Purpose
"Your kingdom come, your will be done, on earth as it is in heaven."

3. God's Provision
"Give us this day our daily bread,"

4. God's Pardon
"and forgive us our debts,"

5. God's Presumption
"as we also have forgiven our debtors."

6. God's Protection
"And lead us not into temptation,"

7. God's Preservation
"but deliver us from evil."

God's due Praise
"Our Father in heaven, hallowed be your name."
First, Jesus tells us to pray to God who is our Father in heaven. He tells us to focus on giving praise and glory to God the Father by specifically calling out one area of importance: His name. God's name is not considered holy in this world. People all over use His name in vain or in profanity. Those who use "OMG" may even be causing other Christians to stumble when they read it. Even if the person saying it means "Oh My Gosh," the person reading it may read, "Oh My God." It is too slippery of a slope so I have chosen to not use OMG, ever, and I also have banned it on my social media pages as profanity. It is that important.

God's Purpose
"Your kingdom come, your will be done, on earth as it is in heaven."
The second part is regarding God's purpose. If we want to follow Jesus, He is clear that He wants us to pray that God's desires will be done here on earth just like it is in heaven. This would mean God's kingdom would come! What a blessed thing to pray for! It is what we all hope for. We want God's plan and purpose to be fulfilled so that we might see Jesus and glorify Him all the more! Come Jesus, come!

God's Provision
"Give us this day our daily bread"
The third part, God's provision, seems almost monotonous compared to the first two. We are speaking to a holy God who has a major plan and mission, yet He loves us so dearly that He tells us it is okay to ask for what we need. "Daily bread" is a symbol for our needs. He knows we are dust. Psalm 103:14 (ESV) says, *"For he knows our frame; he remembers that we are dust."*

Doesn't this make your heart happy? It does mine. We are fragile, and the Almighty Creator of the Universe cares deeply for our needs. To Him they could be almost silly, as He has far more important things to attend to. I love that He loves us, and reminds us to not worry or be anxious about it, because He knows we would be.

> *"And why are you anxious about clothing? Consider the lilies of the field, how they grow: they neither toil nor spin, yet I tell you, even Solomon in all his glory was not arrayed like one of these."* (Matthew 6:28-29 ESV)

God's Pardon
"and forgive us our debts,"

It is an honor and special privilege to come before God, humbly bow before Him, and repent. The fourth part of this example prayer given by Jesus is a clear call to confession. R.C. Sproul stated in his teaching series on "Repentance" that "Repentance is not just turning to something, it's turning from something." When we turn to Jesus and follow Him as our Lord and Savior, turning from our sins, confessing them to Him, and asking Him for His pardon is an important part of our daily walk with Him. I have found that my motives also need forgiveness as do my actions. Clearly and specifically calling out transgressions, even in motive, is an important part of prayer life.

> *"Come now, let us reason together, says the Lord: though your sins are like scarlet, they shall be as white as snow; though they are red like crimson, they shall become like wool."*
> (Isaiah 1:18 ESV)

God's Presumption
"as we also have forgiven our debtors."
God has rightfully presumed that since He has forgiven us, we need to do the same as noted in the fifth part of the Lord's Prayer. Jesus is always quick to flip something onto the other side, and it is no different with forgiveness. While we must confess our sins and ask God to forgive us, we must also forgive others. This can be the much harder portion of this dichotomy. He knew it would be difficult for us. It is one reason why so much of the Bible focuses on love and how we are supposed to treat each other. Forgiving others in our daily prayer may sound hard, but I know that, from experience, it goes a long way toward training us how to love far better than we ever could, and it helps to calm the soul when wronged.

> *"For if you forgive others their trespasses, your heavenly Father will also forgive you, but if you do not forgive others their trespasses, neither will your Father forgive your trespasses."*
> (Matthew 6:14-15 ESV)

God's Protection
"And lead us not into temptation,"
The sixth part of Jesus' prayer model reminds us to ask God to protect us from temptation. It is remarkable to me how often I forget to pray about this. Temptation is all around us, every moment, of every day. Jesus tells us we need to be mindful of it and ask God to be gracious by not allowing it to happen. Think about how often God uses temptation to test and prove His children. Think about Job and how God allowed Satan to tempt Job to curse God. Jesus was allowed to be led into temptation by Satan when he was tempted for

171

40 days and nights in the wilderness. While God does not tempt us, He allows Satan to in order to test us like gold being refined in the fire.

> *"Let no one say when he is tempted, "I am being tempted by God," for God cannot be tempted with evil, and he himself tempts no one."* (James 1:13 ESV)

> *"No temptation has overtaken you that is not common to man. God is faithful, and he will not let you be tempted beyond your ability, but with the temptation he will also provide the way of escape, that you may be able to endure it."*
> (1 Corinthians 10:13 ESV)

God's Preservation

"but deliver us from evil."

The final and seventh part of the Lord's Prayer tells us to ask God to keep evil from us, or in some translations *"deliver us from the evil one."* This is something I fear many of us forget to do. Based on what the Bible tells us, I believe that we will all be shocked at what has been going on behind the scenes in the spiritual realm that we are unable to see right now. Prayer for the preservation of His people and the protection from evil should be something we pray often about and ask others to pray over us as well.

> *"But the Lord is faithful. He will establish you and guard you against the evil one."* (2 Thessalonians 3:3 ESV)

> *"Put on the whole armor of God, that you may be able to stand against the schemes of the devil. For we do not wrestle against flesh and blood, but against the rulers, against the authorities, against the cosmic powers over this present darkness, against the spiritual forces of evil in the heavenly places."*
> (Ephesians 6:11-12 ESV)

The Doxology

In some translations you will see the addition of what is considered the Protestant Doxology as the ending of verse 13 in Matthew 6:13, "For yours is the kingdom and the power and the glory, forever. Amen." It is debated as to when this was added and if it was ever in any original early manuscripts. Most scholars believe it was added in as part of the prayer to round it out. Bible scholars finally agreed that the ending doxology was never in the earliest Greek manuscripts. For this reason, it will not be discussed here further, but you are welcome to use it in your prayer life.

Reciting of the Lord's Prayer

Memorizing scripture is a great way to meditate on His Word and also a means to remember it when there is no Bible at hand. Some churches have chosen to use the Lord's Prayer in their service as a corporate recitation or reading. This form of repetition allows the congregants to memorize this important scripture. The downside to this is that many church-goers now think that this is exactly what you should pray. Rather than talk to God, they recite the Lord's Prayer as a sort of magically perfect prayer that trumps all other prayer.

Please remember the context and that Jesus was sharing an example of how to pray and what to pray for. It can be a blessing to use His prayer as a guide to pray in your own way. I believe this is the idea Jesus was sharing with us when He gave us the beautiful passage that we now refer to as "The Lord's Prayer."

Praying for Everything

In Christian circles, prayer requests often surround people asking each other to pray for bad things to go away: pray for my hurting back, pray for my pending surgery, pray that God would remove the cancer, pray that my child would get better, pray for my sister's dog's rash. They almost seem irrational and petty when compared to the things that the early church prayed for as seen in the New Testament.

In the letters of the New Testament we see prayer mainly for believers to grow in Christ and to become more strong in Jesus. They prayed for people to become more like Jesus. Prayer surrounded kingdom-building rather than solely focusing on personal needs. The requests of the early church were of lasting importance, not only fleeting needs, which we see in Scripture, but in slim proportion to kingdom-building. Today, the pendulum seems to have swung the other way. As I sit in small groups, I hear far more personal requests than kingdom-building requests. The men and women in the Bible prayed for wisdom to do God's will, that the Holy Spirit would fill them, and that their love for each other would grow. Prayers surrounded courage to share their faith and that they would have hope that overflows by the Holy Spirit's power.

This is not to say that you are not supposed to pray for everything and anything. God desires our communion with Him, and He delights in you. My only encouragement here is that we try to defer to God's will more and more as we abide in Him and mature in our relationship with Him.

174

The Secret Ending

How important is it for you to end every prayer in the name of Jesus? Do you feel almost superstitious if you just say Amen? I know I do at times. It has been drilled into my Christian education from early childhood to always use a phrase that goes something like:

"In Jesus' name, Amen."

"I ask these things in the name of Jesus, Amen."

"In the Name of the Father, and of the Son, and of the Holy Spirit. Amen."

Ending prayers this way comes from the passage in John 14.

"Whatever you ask in my name, this I will do, that the Father may be glorified in the Son. If you ask me anything in my name, I will do it." (John 14:13-14 ESV)

What does it mean to ask for something in someone else's name? When you do anything in the name of something or someone else, it commands that you have the backed authority of that thing or name to do so. Here are a few common examples:

- "We did the new surgery in the name of science."
- "Stop! In the name of the law!"
- "We got married in the name of love."
- "I pray these things in Jesus' name!"

Praying by the authority of Jesus is an important distinction to make between prayers by Christians and prayers by non-Christians. If you are *in Jesus* (aka saved,) then you already have the authority and you have access, direct access, to God! The second half of James 5:16 (ESV) says, *"The prayer of a righteous person has great power as it is working."* This verse can also be translated as "The effective prayer of a righteous person has great power." Praying in the name of Jesus, may often be taken literally by Christians as some sort of secret ending that must be uttered, otherwise the prayer might not be heard or answered. How could that be true?

I do not believe that God would be so little as to say, "Now children, if you do not end every prayer this way, I just won't listen." This is something we must remove from our minds. My iconoclastic heart tells me that stating "In Jesus' name" after every single prayer is something man has made bigger than it was meant to be.

Think this through with me: You are saved. You are now *in* Christ Jesus. Your old self is gone and the new version of you is here. You are a new creation who is under the lordship of Jesus. You are His and He is yours. You were adopted into His family and you now have that authority whether you state it out loud or not.

This means that *every* prayer you pray is in the name of Jesus because *you* are in Jesus. Please, my friend, let go of your old superstitions and rest in the assurance that you are sealed with the Holy Spirit and fully and completely have the backed authority in Jesus when you pray to God. Praise Jesus!

CHAPTER 19

ATTRIBUTES OF GOD

Great is our Lord, and abundant in power;
his understanding is beyond measure.
Psalm 147:5 ESV

God has revealed to us parts of who He is in the Bible. We have to assume it is not *all* of who He is because that could never be contained in one small book. We are blessed to have what He has chosen to reveal to us in His communicable and incommunicable attributes. Communicable is often used when talking about diseases that easily spread from one person to another. It may also be used to describe how information passes between people, namely in marketing, and how a company is able to best create a communicable campaign. As it pertains to God's attributes, or personality traits, the word communicable means we, as humans, are able to share these traits.

Communicable attributes are those traits we are able to share with God such as love, understanding, reasoning, knowledge, justice, mercy, grace, rationality, anger, goodness, wisdom, and kindness among others. The incommunicable attributes of God are those that belong only to Him. They are not something we are able to possess. They are distinctly what makes God, God.

Incommunicable Attributes of God

The following is a list of God's incommunicable attributes along with verses so you can pray and meditate on the majesty of who God is. Please note that several verses are used multiple times as they may apply to multiple attributes.

All Knowing - Omniscient

1 John 3:20 ESV
"for whenever our heart condemns us, God is greater than our heart, and he knows everything."

Hebrews 4:13 ESV
"And no creature is hidden from his sight, but all are naked and exposed to the eyes of him to whom we must give account."

Romans 11:33 ESV
"Oh, the depth of the riches and wisdom and knowledge of God! How unsearchable are his judgments and how inscrutable his ways!"

Romans 16:27 ESV
"to the only wise God be glory forevermore through Jesus Christ! Amen."

All Powerful - Omnipotent

Genesis 1-6 ESV – The Creation Story

Psalm 33:9 ESV
"For he spoke, and it came to be; he commanded, and it stood firm."

Isaiah 40:28 ESV
"Have you not known? Have you not heard? The Lord is the everlasting God, the Creator of the ends of the earth. He does not faint or grow weary; his understanding is unsearchable."

Isaiah 46:10 ESV
"declaring the end from the beginning and from ancient times things not yet done, saying, 'My counsel shall stand, and I will accomplish all my purpose,'"

All Places at All Times - Everywhere - Omnipresent

Psalm 139:7-12 ESV

> 7 *"Where shall I go from your Spirit?*
> *Or where shall I flee from your presence?*
> 8 *If I ascend to heaven, you are there!*
> *If I make my bed in Sheol, you are there!*
> 9 *If I take the wings of the morning*
> *and dwell in the uttermost parts of the sea,*
> 10 *even there your hand shall lead me,*
> *and your right hand shall hold me.*
> 11 *If I say, "Surely the darkness shall cover me,*
> *and the light about me be night,"*
> 12 *even the darkness is not dark to you;*
> *the night is bright as the day,*
> *for darkness is as light with you."*

Jeremiah 23:24 ESV

> *"Can a man hide himself in secret places so that I cannot see him?*
> *declares the Lord. Do I not fill heaven and earth? declares the Lord."*

Holy - Set Apart - Perfect

Psalm 99:5 ESV

> *"Exalt the Lord our God; worship at his footstool! Holy is he!"*

Psalm 71:22 ESV

> *"I will also praise you with the harp for your faithfulness, O my*
> *God; I will sing praises to you with the lyre, O Holy One of Israel."*

Isaiah 6:3 ESV

> *"And one called to another and said: "Holy, holy, holy is the Lord*
> *of hosts; the whole earth is full of his glory!"*

1 Peter 1:16 ESV

> *"since it is written, "You shall be holy, for I am holy."*

Immaterial - Spirit - No Physical Form

John 4:24 ESV

"God is spirit, and those who worship him must worship in spirit and truth."

Luke 24:39 ESV

"See my hands and my feet, that it is I myself. Touch me, and see. For a spirit does not have flesh and bones as you see that I have."

Immutable - Unchanging

Malachi 3:6 ESV

"For I the Lord do not change; therefore you, O children of Jacob, are not consumed."

James 1:17 ESV

"Every good gift and every perfect gift is from above, coming down from the Father of lights, with whom there is no variation or shadow due to change."

Hebrews 13:8 ESV

"Jesus Christ is the same yesterday and today and forever."

Infinite - Eternal - Without Limit of Time

Genesis 21:33 ESV

"Abraham planted a tamarisk tree in Beersheba and called there on the name of the Lord, the Everlasting God."

Deuteronomy 33:27a ESV

"The eternal God is your dwelling place, and underneath are the everlasting arms."

Isaiah 40:28 ESV

"Have you not known? Have you not heard? The Lord is the everlasting God, the Creator of the ends of the earth. He does not faint or grow weary; his understanding is unsearchable."

Psalm 90:2 ESV
> *"Before the mountains were brought forth, or ever you had formed the earth and the world, from everlasting to everlasting you are God."*

Psalm 102:24–27 ESV
> 24 *"O my God," I say, "take me not away*
> *in the midst of my days—*
> *you whose years endure*
> *throughout all generations!"*
> 25 *Of old you laid the foundation of the earth,*
> *and the heavens are the work of your hands.*
> 26 *They will perish, but you will remain;*
> *they will all wear out like a garment.*
> *You will change them like a robe, and they will pass away,*
> 27 *but you are the same, and your years have no end."*

Self-existent - Uncaused Who Always Existed

Psalm 90:2 ESV
> *"Before the mountains were brought forth, or ever you had formed the earth and the world, from everlasting to everlasting you are God."*

Psalm 93:2 ESV
> *"Your throne is established from of old; you are from everlasting."*

Revelation 1:8 ESV
> *"I am the Alpha and the Omega," says the Lord God, "who is and who was and who is to come, the Almighty."*

Self-sufficient - Not Dependent on Anything

Acts 17:24-25 ESV
> *"The God who made the world and everything in it, being Lord of heaven and earth, does not live in temples made by man, nor is he served by human hands, as though he needed anything, since he himself gives to all mankind life and breath and everything."*

181

Sovereign - In Charge and in Control Over Everything

1 Timothy 6:15 ESV
> *"which he will display at the proper time—he who is the blessed and only Sovereign, the King of kings and Lord of lords,"*

Isaiah 46:10 ESV
> *"declaring the end from the beginning and from ancient times things not yet done, saying, 'My counsel shall stand, and I will accomplish all my purpose,'"*

Romans 9:19-21 ESV
> *"You will say to me then, "Why does he still find fault? For who can resist his will?" But who are you, O man, to answer back to God? Will what is molded say to its molder, "Why have you made me like this?" Has the potter no right over the clay, to make out of the same lump one vessel for honorable use and another for dishonorable use?"*

Job 42:2 ESV
> *"I know that you can do all things, and that no purpose of yours can be thwarted."*

Transcendent - Without Limit of Space or Time

2 Timothy 1:9 ESV
> *"who saved us and called us to a holy calling, not because of our works but because of his own purpose and grace, which he gave us in Christ Jesus before the ages began,"*

Psalm 139:7-10 ESV
> *7 "Where shall I go from your Spirit?*
> *Or where shall I flee from your presence?*
> *8 If I ascend to heaven, you are there!*
> *If I make my bed in Sheol, you are there!*
> *9 If I take the wings of the morning*
> *and dwell in the uttermost parts of the sea,*
> *10 even there your hand shall lead me,*
> *and your right hand shall hold me."*

Unique - None Like Him

Isaiah 55:8-9 ESV

8 "For my thoughts are not your thoughts,
neither are your ways my ways, declares the Lord.
9 For as the heavens are higher than the earth,
so are my ways higher than your ways
and my thoughts than your thoughts."

Isaiah 43:10 ESV

"You are my witnesses," declares the Lord, "and my servant
whom I have chosen, that you may know and believe me and
understand that I am he. Before me no god was formed, nor
shall there be any after me."

Isaiah 44:6-7 ESV

6 "Thus says the Lord, the King of Israel
    and his Redeemer, the Lord of hosts:
"I am the first and I am the last;
    besides me there is no god.
7 Who is like me? Let him proclaim it.
    Let him declare and set it before me,
since I appointed an ancient people.
    Let them declare what is to come, and what will happen."

CHAPTER 20

CHURCH INVOLVEMENT

"They went out from us, but they were not of us;
for if they had been of us, they would have continued with us.
But they went out, that it might become plain
that they all are not of us."
1 John 2:19 ESV

"A church alive is worth the drive." I have heard that quote too many times to count. My heart wants to believe this, but I know my heart too well. I know that people need people. People desire to feel good and feel loved. They were created by God with a need for community. Without community, depression sets in, and it is now being said that community is the number one thing that keeps us alive the longest. Dr. Emma Seppala of Stanford Medicine published an article in 2014 that stated,

> "One landmark study showed that lack of social connection is a greater detriment to health than obesity, smoking and high blood pressure.

> "On the other hand, strong social connection:

> - leads to a 50% increased chance of longevity
> - strengthens your immune system (research by Steve Cole shows that genes impacted by loneliness also code for immune function and inflammation)
> - helps you recover from disease faster
> - may even lengthen your life!

"People who feel more connected to others have lower levels of anxiety and depression. Moreover, studies show they also have higher self-esteem, greater empathy for others, are more trusting and cooperative and, as a consequence, others are more open to trusting and cooperating with them. In other words, social connectedness generates a positive feedback loop of social, emotional and physical well-being.

"Unfortunately, the opposite is also true for those who lack social connectedness. Low levels of social connection are associated with declines in physical and psychological health as well as a higher likelihood for antisocial behavior that leads to further isolation."

The "landmark study" Dr. Seppala was referencing was a study done by the Department of Epidemiology, University of Michigan, Ann Arbor entitled Social Relationships and Health by JS House, KR Landis, D Umberson.

Human connection is so important for both psychosocial and physiological well-being, that it is no wonder the church can often be the place people go to in order to obtain connection. We see the phenomenon of surges in church attendance whenever a natural disaster or widespread tragic event takes place. Being a part of a "feel-good" and happy church often outweighs a church that convicts and asks people to grow and change.

This quote about finding a good church would be more accurately worded, "A church that makes me smile, is worth the extra mile." The original quote is a good one, but the issue with driving far out of your community to find a good church is not ideal. Being in community means being *in* the community. If you are even 30 minutes away, any number of things may come up preventing you from serving or even attending your church.

It is often advised by pastors to find a church that is around 15 minutes or less from your home. If you live in a rural area, that may be a challenge and is the exception, not the rule. Being a part of your local church is not optional. God did not design us to live out our Christian service to Him alone. He created us out of His own overflowing love within the Trinity. There are three things to consider when you plug into a good local church: Sunday attendance, connecting in smaller groups, and serving in at least one area.

The Service - Corporate Worship

Church is a place to hear the Word of God and participate in corporate worship. If you are at a good church, with a pastor who is dedicated to preaching God's word and not their own, then you will be in good hands. The message that is preached from the pulpit each weekend is usually worked out by the pastor in a quarterly or annual curriculum. When you miss a week, you will miss part of his message, and you also miss valuable instruction, encouragement, and conviction. Worshiping together as a larger congregation is part of what God calls us to do. We are to sing together, learn together, and commune together.

> *"And let us consider how to stir up one another to love and good works, not neglecting to meet together, as is the habit of some, but encouraging one another, and all the more as you see the Day drawing near."* (Hebrews 10:24-25 ESV)

> *"All Scripture is breathed out by God and profitable for teaching, for reproof, for correction, and for training in righteousness,"* (Timothy 3:16 ESV)

Small Groups - Fellowship and Discipleship

Attending the main church service is an important part of the Christian life, but it can be very easy to get lost or be incognito for months or even years if you only attend on Sunday. I know when I am feeling down, I can sneak in the back door, sit down, listen to the sermon, then sneak out before anyone knows I was even there. This is not wise, and this temptation is something I have to work against. I know friends who attend larger churches just so they can "blend in" and not get too involved.

Attending church this way is not what God intended when He asked us to have fellowship with one another. Try to get involved in at least one meeting that happens outside of the normal Sunday service. It may be a weekly Bible study group or home fellowship group that meets to discuss the sermon. It may even be a group of people who enjoy the same hobbies gathering frequently to share life together. Smaller groups provide the perfect opportunity to be in meaningful community with other disciples. God blesses us with relationships where people care about us and provide us with encouragement, discipleship, prayer, accountability, and support.

> *"For where two or three are gathered in my name, there am I among them."* (Matthew 18:20 ESV)

> *"Iron sharpens iron, and one man sharpens another."* (Proverbs 27:17 ESV)

Service - Gifts and Offerings of Time

Once you are committed to attending church every Sunday, and are plugged into a good smaller group for fellowship and discipleship, it is time to look for an area to serve at your church. The best way to do this is to look around. What is not getting done or needs help? What strengths do you possess that could bless your church? Don't overthink this at first. It is easy to think you will swoop in and be a God-send for your church. Don't let Satan destroy a good deed through a puffed up spirit. Consider lowly tasks. Remember, your church is your home, not just a place you go. The following are some ideas for you to consider to start serving unofficially in general service to your church:

General Service Ideas

- When you are in the bathroom, wipe down the counter.
- If you are in a stall and it is messy, clean it up.
- If you walk by a piece of discarded trash on the floor, pick it up and throw it away.
- If the pillows on the couch in the foyer are squished, fluff them up and put them back in place.
- After service, consider cleaning up around your area by picking up leftover programs and putting back pens and Bibles in the pew-backs or chairs.
- If you see an overflowing trashcan, find out where the trash bags are and where they put the trash, then simply change the bag and throw out the trash.
- Ask if there is any gardening you can help with.

- If a kid is crying, help him or her find their mom.

- Help an elderly person get from their car to their seat in the church.

- If you hear of someone whose car broke down, offer a ride to church.

- Bring a meal to a church member in need.

- Look for pastoral requests and do them, such as helping pass out fliers, or staying after church to help put up or take down seasonal decorations.

- Head over to the children's outdoor area and tidy up.

You get the idea.

Once you get in the mindset of viewing your church property as your home and the community as your family, you will start to see areas to serve all around you. After you get the hang of general service to your church, you will want to look for a specific service area that you can support.

Specific Service Ideas
This list is not a checklist. Please consider using this list as an opportunity to serve from the heart.

- Become a teacher/helper in the children's ministry.

- Join the women's/men's ministry team.

- Become an usher.

- Try out for the worship team.

- Become a leader in the youth group.

- Join the prayer team.

- Join the clean-up team.
- Join the outreach team.
- Join the missions team.
- Join the jail ministry.
- Sign up to be a part of the meal train for those in need.
- Ask how to help with church mailings by stuffing envelopes or helping with volunteer admin work.
- Join any team your church has that your talents support.
- Start a new ministry with the support of your pastor that is lacking in your church.

Specific service areas are those where your gifts and talents can be utilized to serve others. Sometimes they are tasks anyone could do, but you realize there's a need that you could service well. Not every need is a calling though. Some of us want to help and whenever people share a service need, your first instinct is to jump at it. I encourage you to start with the general service ideas first and then pick one or maybe two areas of service that you feel you could contribute to. Do not overwhelm yourself. Everything we do, we have the honor of doing for Jesus!

> *"Whatever you do, work heartily, as for the Lord and not for men, knowing that from the Lord you will receive the inheritance as your reward. You are serving the Lord Christ."*
> (Colossians 3:23-24 ESV)

> *"As each has received a gift, use it to serve one another, as good stewards of God's varied grace:"* (1 Peter 4:10 ESV)

*"For as in one body we have many members, and the members
do not all have the same function, so we, though many, are
one body in Christ, and individually members one of another."*
(Romans 12:4-5 ESV)

The basic idea is to get involved. Your church is your home and your family. Be present. Be mindful. Share life with your church family. I remember being asked a question many years ago that stumped me. I would like to ask you the same one. Really think about this. "If you died today, would your church feel a hole where you once were?" For me, at the time, the answer was "no." In some regards, today, that answer is still "no" because the area I serve I truly feel anyone could pick up the baton and keep going. The question is a good one to reflect on, but it is not saying you must fill a big role in your church.

For me, I pay close attention to the smaller needs that I might help with when I am there. My service area is our "Book Spot" where we highlight recommended books that I keep stocked and fill with new ones. It is a perfect specific service job for me because I love reading and I love books. Because of my traveling and life duties, it allows me to serve in the capacity I am able to in this season of my life. In my mind I can see a future me leading Bible studies and teaching women in a larger capacity, but for now God has me where He needs me and I am perfectly fine with that.

What is your commitment today? Consider something like this: "I commit to attending church regularly, getting plugged into a small fellowship group, and finding an area I can be of service to my church."

FINAL THOUGHTS

God has blessed me in ways I may never comprehend, and I know He has blessed you, too! This was a hard book for me to write, and I am sure it was a hard book to read. As I went back and forth with my theological editors, one main pain point kept arising. How can I connect with a reader who finds the contents of this book a burden too heavy to bear? My delivery tends to be black and white in a world where subtle grays are often found.

I have prayed long and hard that God would draw exactly the right people to this book. I have rested in the assurance that it is not my job to convert people or to convince anyone of the truths found in the Bible. My job is simply to deliver those truths to those willing to hear. It is the job of the Holy Spirit to draw people to Him and to convince people of their sin and their need to get right with God.

When I was going through the process of being drawn, or more aptly put, dragged to Christ, I remember the process well. It was fascinating to me how easily I released my human struggles and domestications of God. I remember my mind thinking, "Wow, Jen, you're accepting hard truths that only months ago you would have argued with or balked at as antiquated." It was unlike me for sure. God was working on my heart. He was taking down my defenses and allowing my mind and heart to be moldable and teachable. It was a season of searching and questioning. Having gone through this process, I know that it is only through the work of the Holy Spirit that anyone is saved. Do you find yourself in a season of seeking true truths?

At the time of my conversion I was moonlighting between two churches. I was attending my long-time church that had been completely upended and under all new leadership. It was a good church with good people and easy-to-listen-to preaching and teaching. I would attend Sunday mornings at that "long-time" church and on Saturday nights I went to a "new-to-me" church that several of my old friends and mentors started to attend.

There was a stark difference in what I heard each weekend. On Saturday, at the "new-to-me" church, I heard hard truths and major conviction that had a call to action. The pastor covered topics I had never heard before, during my entire experience in the Protestant church. On Sunday, at my "long-time" church, it was back to normal, with topical preaching that made everyone feel good. What I noticed after each service was that the conversations people had at each church were nothing alike.

After the Saturday night service, at the "new-to-me" church people were deep in theological discussions, sharpening each other and spurring each other on. On Sunday morning, at my "long-time" church, the conversation steered in the direction of where to go to lunch and how the kids and family were doing. It was a difference of spiritually alive verses socially alive.

My mind and soul was famished at my "long-time" church. When I went to the "new-to-me" church it was like having a tall, cold glass of water after being stranded in a hot, dry desert for years. I drank it in. Every ounce. I wanted more. I started to attend more of this new church's curriculum. I found past sermons from eight years back online and listened to every single one over the course of about six months. I would listen to three to four sermons every single day. I turned that tall glass of water into a steady fire hose of learning. My soul was desperate for answers and I had no way of turning back. It was as if I had no other choice. That is the call of the Holy Spirit. It is inescapable and irresistible!

If you read this book, and it made an impact on your life, I imagine that you may be one of two people, but perhaps others were impacted as well, and for that I am grateful:

- You may be a Christian who may have let the domestication of God infiltrate your life a little too much and now you desire and thirst for more of Jesus and the true truths He has to offer.

- You may be a person who has always identified with Christianity, but now, after reading this book, feel that maybe you need to reevaluate your walk with God knowing the Holy Spirit is working on you even now.

Again, if you read this book, and the above two are not you, I am glad this book has helped you. My main goal in writing it was to help even one person get one step closer to Jesus no matter where they are with their walk. If that is you, PRAISE JESUS!

When a Christian, or someone who identifies strongly with Christianity, takes steps to undomesticate God, they are collectively raising their view of God, examining their own faith, and discovering the true reality of salvation through the lordship of Jesus.

God has done a profound work in my life and my heart that has affected the outpouring of my actions. It has brought me to my knees, and filled my heart with joy knowing I am privileged to have an intimacy with God beyond anything I can share with those here on earth. When you find something so incredible, so awesome, and so radically beautiful, it is impossible not to want that for others. This is what I want for you! This is why I wrote this book. It is the overflow of my heart and I am honored to be able to share my story with you.

Thank you for allowing me to be on this journey with you and for hearing my challenges, how God has revealed Himself to me through His Truth, and of His people who have touched me in my life along the way. It humbles me that you have allowed me to speak into your life and it is my prayer that you would develop a rich spiritual yearning to grow and mature, so that your view of God might match up to how He views Himself.

Blessings to you, dear one, and to God be the glory!

~ Jen O'Sullivan

RECOMMENDED READING

- Andrew Murray "Humility"
- Arthur Bennett "The Valley of Vision"
- A.W. Tozer "The Knowledge of the Holy"
- A.W. Tozer "The Pursuit of God"
- C.S. Lewis "Mere Christianity"
- David Platt "Follow Me"
- Francis Chan "Crazy Love"
- Francis Chan "Forgotten God"
- Gregory Koukl "Tactics"
- Helen L. Taylor "Little Pilgrim's Progress"
- J.I. Packer "Knowing God"
- Jay Adams "The Grand Demonstration"
- Jerry Bridges "The Disciplines of Grace"
- Jerry Bridges "The Pursuit of Holiness"
- John Foxe "Foxe's Book of Martyrs"
- John MacArthur "The Gospel According to Jesus"
- John Piper "Desiring God"
- Kevin Deyoung "The Hole in our Holiness"
- Kyle Idleman "Gods at War"
- Kyle Idleman "Not a Fan"
- Lee Strobel "The Case for Christ"
- Mike Fabarez "Lifelines for Tough Times"
- Paul David Tripp "Instruments in the Redeemer's Hands"
- RC Sproul "Chosen by God"
- RC Sproul "The Holiness of God"
- Timothy Keller "The Reason for God"

RESOURCES

FREE DOWNLOADS
www.31oils.com/UGfree

Jen's Blogs
www.HolyJustLove.com
www.AnExcellentWife.com

Blue Letter Bible (Strong's Concordance)
www.BlueLetterBible.org

Church Finder
www.9marks.org/church-search

New City Catechism
www.newcitycatechism.com

The Gospel Coalition
www.thegospelcoalition.org

Book and Audio Resources
www.ligonier.org

Discount Bibles and Books
www.christianbook.com

How to Share the Gospel Message
www.sharetheumbrella.com

Bible Apps
- YouVersion Bible App
- Tecarta Bible App
- Blue Letter Bible App
- Logos Bible Study Tools App

to God be the glory